SECESSION DEBATED

SECESSION DEBATED

Georgia's Showdown in 1860

Edited by
WILLIAM W. FREEHLING
CRAIG M. SIMPSON

New York   Oxford
OXFORD UNIVERSITY PRESS
1992

Oxford University Press

Oxford   New York   Toronto
Delhi   Bombay   Calcutta   Madras   Karachi
Kuala Lumpur   Singapore   Hong Kong   Tokyo
Nairobi   Dar es Salaam   Cape Town
Melbourne   Auckland

and associated companies in
Berlin   Ibadan

Copyright © 1992 by William W. Freehling, Craig M. Simpson

Published by Oxford University Press, Inc.,
198 Madison Avenue, New York, New York 10016-4314

Oxford is a registered trademark of Oxford University Press

Library of Congress Cataloging-in-Publication Data
Secession debated : Georgia's showdown in 1860 /
edited by William W. Freehling and Craig M. Simpson.
p.   cm.   Includes bibliographical references.
ISBN 0-19-507944-2 (cloth)
ISBN 0-19-507945-0 (paper)
1. Secession.   2. Georgia—Politics and government—Civil War, 1861-1865.
I. Freehling, William W., 1935- .   II. Simpson, Craig, M., 1942- .
E459.S43   1992
973.7'13—dc20   92-10695

9 8 7 6 5 4

Printed in the United States of America
on acid-free paper

For

Alison
and
Peggy

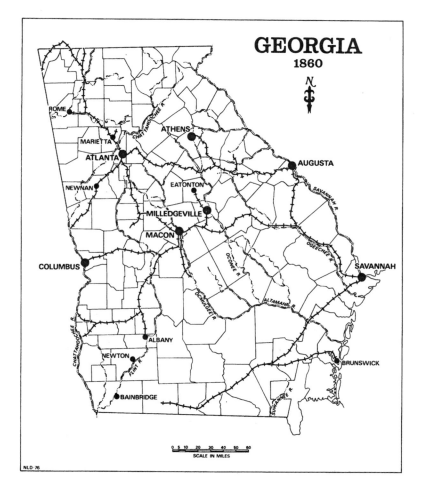

Source: Michael P. Johnson. Toward a Patriarchal Republic: The Secession of Georgia *(Baton Rouge: Louisiana State University Press, 1977).*

Introduction

The critical northern antebellum debate matched Abraham Lincoln against Stephen A. Douglas in 1858. The parallel southern confrontation, matching secessionists against Unionists, took place in Georgia's antebellum capital, Milledgeville, during the third week of November, 1860. At that moment of southern decision, Lincoln had just been elected to the presidency. In response to this "Black Republican" triumph, South Carolina's skittish secessionists moved towards precipitous action. South Carolina governor William Gist, anticipating Lincoln's victory, had called a legislative session. The imminently convening legislature was expected to summon a December state convention, which likely would swiftly enact a secession ordinance.

In mid-November, 1860, while South Carolina's secession looked inevitable, the other fourteen slave states' response seemed uncertain. Ever since 1787, most Southerners had treasured the Union. Ever since the Nullification Crisis of 1832–33, when the South's hero, President Andrew Jackson, had

faced down South Carolina's idol, John C. Calhoun, most Southerners had been wary of South Carolina's precipitancy.

South Carolina's hastiness was again an issue in 1860–61.
Whereas most South Carolinians feared that President-elect
Lincoln might menace slavery immediately after his inauguration on March 4, 1861, most other Southerners saw no clear
and present danger. Secessionists' opponents conceded that
northern interference with the return of fugitive slaves must
be resisted. Unionists also conceded that Lincoln hated slavery,
that he hoped to put the institution on the road to ultimate
extinction, and that he opposed slavery's expansion into federal
territories.

But few Southerners, Unionists pointed out, wished to mi-
grate into then-held United States territories. Lincoln's Republican Party controlled neither the Congress nor the
Supreme Court. As for the President-elect, while he rejected
slavery's spread into new territory, he renounced federal intervention in old slave states. If Lincoln violated that pledge
of nonintervention, and if the Congress and Supreme Court
allowed a presidential abolitionist invasion, secession must ensue. Furthermore, unless alternate resistances stopped northern interference with the federal Fugitive Slave Law, secession
might be necessary. But why not initially try less dangerous
forms of resistance, both to deter Lincoln from unconstitutional
interference and to force northern compliance with the Fugitive
Slave Law?

That question was usually deemed unanswerable in the
eight northernmost southern states, comprising the so-called
Upper South. Inside this least tropical fraction of the Slave
South lived only 41 percent of southern slaves but 67 percent
of southern whites.[1] For South Carolina to overcome this south-

1. All statistics in this Introduction were derived from Francis A. Walker,
comp., *The Statistics of the Population of the United States* (Washington, 1870),
and from United States Bureau of the Census, *A Century of Population Growth;*

ern white majority, the precipitating state's six sister Lower South states would have to secede. Then Upper South Unionists might be driven to the choice which they both dreaded and thought need never be made: Were they slaveholders, standing with the Lower South, or Unionists, standing with the North? If civil war ensued, the Upper South would be the more compelled to choose.

Among Lower South states, Mississippi and Alabama and Florida seemed likely to follow South Carolina's lead. Texas's and Louisiana's decisions seemed more uncertain. But the critical uncertainty concerned Georgia. Ten years earlier, after the Compromise of 1850, the famous Georgia triumvirate of Alexander Stephens, Howell Cobb, and Robert Toombs had led a triumphant unionist state campaign, shattering South Carolina secessionists' already slim prospects.

Now in November, 1860, Georgians' appropriately named Empire State could demoralize any Lower South nation, if they refused to join it. Georgia was both an Old South, Atlantic seaboard state and a New South, cotton kingdom. It thus appropriately separated South Carolina/Florida on the sea from the Southwest on the Mississippi. This in-between state contained the second-most acreage of any American state east of the Mississippi (only Virginia included more territory) and the second-most acreage of any Lower South state (only Texas stretched farther). Georgia also had more people, more voters, more slaves, and more slaveholders than any other Lower South state.

But this slaveholders' stronghold also contained a large nonslaveholder majority. More than three in five Georgia voters were nonslaveholders. In addition, two vast Georgia areas contained scarcely a planter: the wiregrass/pine barrens in the southeast and the mountainous region in the north. Between

---

From the First Census of the United States to the Twelfth, 1790–1900 (Washington, 1909).

these sparsely enslaved nonslaveholder regions lay Georgia's heavily enslaved black belt, which, especially in the lush Savannah River valley, rivaled South Carolina in spawning an old-fashioned slaveholders' regime.

If Georgia's 37 percent minority of slaveholders (who tended to favor secession) could not persuade enough of the 63% majority of nonslaveholders (who tended to favor Union), any Southern Confederacy would be imperiled. Secessionists in South Carolina/Florida, separated from secessionists in Mississippi/Alabama, might be overwhelmed by the huge unionist majority in the Upper South. Thus southern eyes turned on tiny Milledgeville in mid-November, 1860, to see where a divided legislature might lead a divided populace.

Milledgeville, geographically in the center of Georgia, epitomized a state and a Slave South with no commanding core. The political village had no important reason to exist except politics; it bordered on neither Georgia's nonslaveholder nor slaveholder strongholds. The town's surrounding environment, awash with rivers and creeks and pockmarked by rolling hills, made efficient road construction impossible. Even after a railroad spur was completed in 1851, successful travel to the capital was cause for congratulations. Indeed, Georgia's railroad boom during the 1850s further marginalized Milledgeville while encouraging Atlanta's imminent significance, not least as the state's capital after the Civil War.[2]

Because small-town state capitals such as Milledgeville were otherwise inconsequential, they were like empty stages, waiting for actors to enliven them. When legislators came to town, performances abounded. Young men preened. Young women dressed and redressed. The militia never failed to drill. But in this age of the spoken word and democratic electioneering, public debate was the treasured spectacle. Georgians

2. James C. Bonner, *Milledgeville: Georgia's Antebellum Capital* (Macon, 1985), pp. 35, 132–35.

came to Milledgeville to witness duels both verbal and physical, to observe and influence decisions affecting life and fortune, and to judge the endless speechifying.

Ostensibly in charge in Milledgeville, in November, 1860, was Governor Joseph E. Brown, a fractious North Georgia politician. The governor's energy and positions tended to please the slaveholders, for no North Georgian so fervently preached that white men, whether slaveholders or nonslaveholders, must keep black "inferiors" enslaved. Compared with other Deep South defenders of slavery, however, Brown owned few slaves. Furthermore, no other slaveholders' champion, except maybe Georgia's United States Senator Robert Toombs, was given to such wild oratory and such uncertain action. Could Joseph E. Brown—could any North Georgian—quite be trusted?

On November 7, the day the Georgia legislature convened and only hours before confirmation of Lincoln's victory arrived in Milledgeville, Governor Brown raised that question again with his Special Message to the legislators. This state paper on the sectional crisis was vintage Brown, both in its dire diagnosis and in its indefinite remedy. No secessionist could outdo Brown's phrase for northern defiance of the federal Fugitive Slave Law: "treason against the Federal Government."[3] Nor could any secessionist fault Brown's explanation of how Abraham Lincoln, by appointing federal officials in the South, could instantly menace slavery. "So soon as the Government shall have passed into Black Republican hands," warned Georgia's governor,

> a portion of our citizens, must, if possible, be bribed into treach-
> ery to their own section, by the allurements of office; or a hungry

3. *Special Message of Gov. Joseph E. Brown, to the Legislature of Georgia, on our Federal Relations, Retaliatory State Legislation, the Right of Secession, etc., November 7th, 1860* (Milledgeville, 1860), p. 9.

swarm of abolition emissaries, must be imported among us as
office holders, to eat out our substance, insult us with their
arrogance, corrupt our slaves, and engender discontent among
them; while they flood the country with inflammatory abolition
documents; and do all in their power, to create in the South, a
state of things which must ultimately terminate in a war of
extermination between the white and black races.[4]

Then, having suggested an alarming problem, Brown proposed a murky solution. He opposed a conference with secessionist South Carolina. He rejected an immediate Georgia
secession ordinance. After hinting that successful secession depended on all fifteen slaveholding states' concurrence, he did
not explain how secessionists could coerce or cajole the tepid
Border South states into revolution. Nor did he explain how
his initial proposed resistances—arming the state, boycotting
northern commerce, seizing alien people or property in Georgia—could deter Lincoln from subversive appointments. Nor
did he explain how his proposals differed from Unionists' preference for resistances short of secession. The governor's Special
Message, in short, both escalated the felt need for revolutionary
remedies and suggested that North Georgians might not meet
revolutionary requirements.

Five days later, on Monday, November 12, two incidents,
simultaneous but unrelated, made revolution seem more necessary but less achievable. First of all, rumors spread of an
alleged slave uprising, on a plantation seven miles from Milledgeville.[5] Second, a state-wide convention of militiamen mus-

4. *Ibid.*, p. 17.
5. Georgia King to Richard Cuyler King, November 13, 1860, Thomas
Butler King Papers, Southern Historical Collection, University of North Carolina Library, Chapel Hill. All the Georgia King letters cited in this Introduction can be found in Box 15 of the Thomas Butler King Papers. This series

tered at the capital. Especially in view of slaves' apparent uprising, conventioneers cheered Governor Brown's oath that for each Georgian injured by Lincolnite coercers, "the heads of two Federal soldiers, should atone for the outrage upon State Sovereignty." But secessionists unhappily noticed that even among the predominantly intransigent militiamen, Unionists blocked unanimity.[6]

Fed up with Joseph E. Brown's only sometimes secessionist rhetoric and fearing the popular sentiment for Union, two secessionists in Georgia's House of Representatives threatened to split the very seals of American republicanism. Hartridge of Chatman and Sprayberry of Catoosa both introduced resolutions aimed at taking Georgia out of the Union by legislative enactment, without waiting for a convention.[7] In the grammar of American republicanism, only the people, assembled in convention, could withdraw their consent to be governed and transfer authority to a new legislature. Now the old legislature had before it resolutions for revolution without a popular vote—for revolution solely by the elite, in a mere legislature assembled.

That Monday night, November 12, Thomas R. R. Cobb, Howell Cobb's deeply respected but less famous younger brother, gave the initial oration in the Milledgeville debate over secession.[8] Cobb's speech established ground rules for the ensuing week of forensic encounters. Leading Georgians would

---

of Georgia King letters forms a priceless eye-witness account, by an informed observer; Georgia King's father, Thomas Butler King, was a state senator and the chairman of the Joint Select Committee of the House and Senate, appointed to deliberate on Brown's Special Message.

6. On the militia convention, see again Georgia King to Richard Cuyler King, November 13, 1860, and *The Macon Daily Telegraph*, November 13, 1860.

7. *The* (Augusta) *Daily Constitutionalist*, November 15, 1860; *The Macon Daily Telegraph*, November 13, 1860; Georgia King to Henry Lord Page King, November 15, 1860.

8. See below, Chapter 1.

offer advice to the legislators not during the legislative sessions but after daily adjournment, at night, in the legislative halls, with both legislators and citizens gathered before them.

Cobb's secessionist oration also re-emphasized the immediate procedural issue. Could the legislature, meeting by day, pass a secession ordinance if the extra-legislative debates, happening at night, established a consensus for secession? T. R. R. Cobb seemed to answer with words which his friends would have later moved the earth to obliterate. He urged that legislators "wait not till the grog stops and crossroads shall send up a discordant voice from a divided people."[9] If the legislative elite stalled until an uncertain public decided, worried this cautious revolutionary, some frustrated secessionist, seizing some sword, might pitch the state into premature civil war.

The next morning, Tuesday, November 13, members of the Georgia House's Standing Committee on the State of the Republic invited Georgia's elite to continue the evening debates which T. R. R. Cobb had initiated. The House Committee called on twenty-four distinguished Georgians, not currently holding legislative seats, to come to Milledgeville and give public advice. The Committee adroitly chose the best representatives of both factions, secessionists and Unionists, thus making nonparticipation difficult.[10]

That night, the secessionists' Robert Toombs, giving the second speech in the Milledgeville debate, could not match

---

9. Cobb's words do not *necessarily* call for a *legislative* Secession Ordinance, and Cobb later claimed any such interpretation "misrepresented" his views, however "*unintentionally*." Cobb to the editors, December, 1860, *The* (Athens Weekly) *Southern Banner*, December 6, 1860. But see "Y" in *The Savannah Daily Republican*, November 21, 1860; *The* (Athens Weekly) *Southern Watchman*, December 5, 1860.

10. The Committee on the State of the Republic of the Georgia House of Representatives to Twenty-four Georgians, November 13, 1860, in *The Macon Daily Telegraph*, November 17, 1860.

T. R. R. Cobb's eloquence but exceeded Cobb's indiscretions.
With Toombs, as with Governor Brown, extravagant posturing
and inconsistent programs were to be expected. Not one to
disappoint, Toombs nominated himself to overcome unionist
caution: "Give me the sword! but if you do not place it in my
hands, before God! *I will take it.*"[11] Visions of such wild seizures
of power were exactly what had impelled T. R. R. Cobb towards
calm legislative action.

Then, after Toombs had concluded, an even wilder assault
on American political orthodoxy was intimated. The crowd
called for a Georgia favorite, the zealous Francis S. Bartow of
Savannah. A former Whig and late blooming secessionist, Bartow gave an extemporaneous and never fully reported speech.
In such a charged environment, however, one Bartow sentence
became notorious. Bartow admitted suggesting "that, under
certain circumstances, it might be necessary for the States of
the South . . . to concentrate their energies and power in a simple form of Republican Government."[12] Bartow here hinted that
to make secession work, a central southern government might
have to possess all authority. So much for another requirement
of American republicanism: power divided between state and
federal governments. The first two evenings of the Milledgeville debate had yielded hints of both dissolution of the Union
without popular referendum and dissolution of Georgia's
government!

Small wonder, then, that the next night, the Unionists'
Alexander H. Stephens announced his intentions to "allay"

11. See below, Chapter 2. While Toombs used the second person in the
printed version of his remarks, we have followed the reports of Georgia King
and Alexander Stephens, who heard the spoken words, that Toombs then used
the first person. See below, p. 75, and Georgia King to Henry Lord Page King,
November 15, 1860. Italics are in the King letter.

12. Francis S. Bartow to the Editor, in *The Savannah Daily Republican*,
November 27, 1860.

strife and "appeal to reason" in "a calm and dispassionate manner."[13] While attributing his presence to yesterday's public invitation, Stephens arrived suitably armed with a major address, obviously considered and reconsidered over many days. Only fools underestimated Stephens when he came to the podium like this, prepared and committed. Yet, his appearance could deceive. Georgia King, daughter of an important state senator, caught Stephens perfectly the previous night, when he sat near her during Toombs's speech: "What a curious looking man he is! His little withered hands in gloves much too large—a face like a mummy—except the bright black eye—and when on the stand, he looked like a little boy."[14]

Stephens was never more the mature seer than in his November 14 evening oration. Challenging Governor Brown's claim that President Lincoln's southern appointments could immediately menace slavery, Stephens pointed out that the Democratic Party controlled the United States Senate and that the Senate must approve all nominations. Turning on Toombs's wanderings of the previous evening, Stephens capitalized on his friend's impulsiveness. As Stephens spoke, Toombs jumped up and down, the perfect foil for a steady strategist. At Stephen's dare to contrast the glories of American government with any other, Toombs blurted out: "England." A few minutes later, he took Stephens's bait that "our Constitution came from the people, . . . and they alone can rightfully unmake it." "I am afraid of conventions," Toombs volunteered. Under the influence of whatever inspiration, Toombs then announced that a state convention would "submit to abolition rule." Finally, Stephens quoted Toombs's preference for seizing the sword and associated that irresponsibility with Thomas Cobb, who had also advised the legislature to act before hearing "from the crossroads and groceries."

13. See below, Chapter 3.
14. Georgia King to Henry Lord Page King, November 15, 1860.

After Stephens finished, Toombs regained his composure. In a gesture frequently recalled by contemporaries and scholars, he urged three cheers for little Aleck: "You have just listened to one of the brightest intellects and purest hearts of Georgia."[15] The cheerleader thus wisely deflected demands for his own response.

Toombs, again wisely, realized that other secessionists would thrive better another night. He moved that the meeting adjourn.[16] But his colleagues refused to leave. Frustrated by how utterly Stephens had trapped Toombs, and appreciating the potentially devastating authority of Stephens's unanswered unionist speech, secessionists demanded the podium. A Savannah judge, Henry R. Jackson, though not expected in Milledgeville,[17] had apparently hurried over, to accept the Georgia House Committee's invitation to speak. When Stephens's supporters denied Judge Jackson the podium, a near riot followed. A secessionist demanded that a unionist state legislator "shut up his throat." When another Unionist seemed to be drawing a gun, this same fireeater threatened to "blow out his brains." Georgia King then summarizes: "Jackson did not get the stand, but spoke from a desk—I confess I did not admire his speech—he ranted terribly—made out an awful case—said we live under the *"blackest* [?] despotism [!] under the sun?!"[18] Neither Jackson's tirade nor Stephens's rejoinder were formally reported. But Jackson later contributed a furious series of public letters, assailing Stephens in near personal terms.[19]

This angry public confrontation more than ever demanded

15. *The Savannah Daily Republican*, November 17, 1860.
16. *Ibid.*
17. Thomas R. R. Cobb to David C. Barrow, undated but early November, 1860, Colonel David C. Barrow Papers, University of Georgia Library, Athens.
18. Georgia King to Henry Lord Page King, November 15, 1860.
19. *Letters from Henry R. Jackson to the Hon. Alex H. Stephens* (Savannah, 1860).

calm legislative decision. It came the next day, Thursday, November 15. Acting on counsel from Georgia's wisest, the House's Standing Committee on the State of the Republic and a Joint Select Committee of the House and Senate both unanimously recommended a convention bill. The bill scheduled a Georgia convention for January 16, 1861, with elections of delegates to take place on January 2. The legislature would approve this bill on November 20, thereby ending the Milledgeville evening speeches. In the interim, the night-time orations would continue. Everyone now knew that the spoken words would become published campaign tracts, useful in the upcoming election for convention delegates.

The compromise language in the convention bill secured temporary unanimity from warring campaigners. On the one hand, the preamble to the bill undercut those few Unionists who opposed all resistance to Lincoln or to northern interference with the Fugitive Slave Law. "The present crisis in our affairs," declared the preamble, "*demands resistance.*"[20] On the other hand, the compromise preamble undercut those secessionists who would enact an immediate *legislative* Secession Ordinance, in their haste to declare secession the only effective resistance. "The sovereign people," conceded the legislature, must determine "the mode, measure and time of . . . resistance."

That Thursday night, November 15, the specter of the Georgia people on January 2nd next, killing secession as the proper resistance, was more than ever in the air. For on the fourth evening of the Milledgeville debate, Benjamin H. Hill gave another stunning unionist speech.[21] The next day, ex-

---

20. For the wording of the preamble, see *The Georgia* (Weekly Macon) *Journal and Messenger,* November 4, 1860.

For the importance of the universal agreement to "resistance," see A. R. Lawton to Robert N. Gourdin, November 20, 1860, Keith Read Collection, University of Georgia Library, Athens.

21. See below, Chapter 4.

Governor Herschel V. Johnson dispatched from Milledgeville a crisp unionist public letter, urging that resistances short of secession must first be tried.[22]

Herschel Johnson and Benjamin Hill, like Alexander Stephens, championed a resistance which went dramatically beyond the famous Georgia Platform of 1850. In that ten-year-old manifesto, the state had pledged some form of "resistance," and should lesser resistances fail, even as "a last resort" secession, if the *federal government* interfered with such slaveholder protections as the Fugitive Slave Law of 1850. Now Johnson, Hill, and Stephens demanded resistance, and even as "a last resort" secession, if the federal government *or the northern states* interfered with the Fugitive Slave Law. By urging an expanded pledge of resistance, the three Unionists mocked secessionists' charge that opponents of secession favored dishonorable "submission." With their strengthened Georgia Platform, Unionists also defied secessionists to show that the "last resort," secession, must be the first resistance deployed.[23]

All in all, Stephens, Johnson, and Hill had dominated the Milledgeville debate's first week too easily for their own good. Overconfident Unionists, upon entering the post-Milledgeville public campaign, would seldom muster passionate effort. Alexander Stephens, the early victor at Milledgeville, would develop a particularly fateful case of inertia.

In contrast, worried secessionists would zealously campaign. Where the Unionists' Stephens, for example, was a host in Milledgeville and almost invisible on subsequent campaign trails, the secessionists' Howell Cobb, having avoided the festival in Milledgeville, would become a force on the hustings.

---

22. See below, Chapter 5.

23. For the wording of the Georgia Platform, see *Debates and Proceedings of the Georgia Convention, 1850* (Milledgeville, 1850), pp. 7–9. For, a further discussion of the Unionists' expansion of the Georgia Platform, see below, Chapter 3, note 11, p. 69.

This shift in momentum first became visible on Monday, November 19, the last night of the Milledgeville debate, when Henry Benning, an ex-Georgia Supreme Court judge, gave a better secessionist speech than the more famous Toombs had mustered.[24]

Judge Benning ridiculed the Unionists' proposed resistance to northern fugitive slave rescues. The real problem, said Benning, even financially, was hardly fugitive slave losses, which accounted for under 2 percent of the southern wealth unfairly drained northward. The graver menace, declared Benning, involved the ever-richer North's ever-greater majority of states. In the near future, Upper South states would sell all their slaves to the Lower South. Meanwhile, the North would gain twenty other states, by populating American territories. Soon the shrinking South, packed with blacks and robbed of dollars, would face abolition by constitutional amendment—and then savage racial warfare.

Momentum shifted further towards secession when Governor Brown, in the climactic polemic emanating from Milledgeville, traded wayward radicalism for determined secessionism. In his public letter of December 7, North Georgia's favorite politician urged nonslaveholders to back slaveholders' revolution, to preserve the Great White Race against Lincoln's alleged menace.[25] Momentum shifted even more on the very day of the election for convention delegates. On that historic January 2, Joseph E. Brown, bringing to mind Toombs's threat to grab the sword

24. See below, Chapter 6. Benning's speech has been misdated in most secondary accounts, for the very good reason that it was mysteriously misdated, in the title of the published version of the speech, as occurring on November 6th. But the publication contains a letter from friends, dated November 19, soliciting a text of the "address which you delivered tonight." Benning's text includes an answer to unionist speeches of the previous week, so it could not have occurred before those speeches. For the proper November 19 date, see also *The Macon Daily Telegraph*, November 22, 27, 1860.

25. See below, Chapter 7.

and T. R. R. Cobb's fear of such hotheads, ordered Georgia militamen to capture Fort Pulaski, the federal installation in Savannah's harbor.[26] The state executive, having now deployed both the sword and the word, could no longer be dismissed as a masquerading cavalier.

The election results revealed that the Governor Browns had overcome the Alexander Stephenses' headstart—but only barely. Approximately 51 percent of Georgia voters favored immediate secession. Because secessionists had secured such a fragile basis for revolution, Brown published the election returns only after the Southern Confederacy was well launched. The governor then erroneously claimed that 58 percent of Georgians had voted to secede.[27]

No matter. First the leaders in Milledgeville had brilliantly debated. Then the people at the crossroads had narrowly decided. On January 19, 1861, the Georgia Convention voted to secede, 166–130. A projected southern confederacy had its Lower South hinge. And now in this, the first collected edition of the Milledgeville debate, posterity has access to a great American verbal showdown.

•

26. Joseph Brown to A. R. Lawton, January 2, 1861, Telamon Cuyler Collection, University of Georgia Library, Athens.

27. See the brilliant analysis in Michael P. Johnson, "A New Look at the Popular Vote for Delegates to the Georgia Secession Convention," *Georgia Historical Quarterly,* 56 (1972), 259–75.

Editorial Procedure

In a series of primary documents, as opposed to a secondary reconstruction of events, the historian does not stand as visibly between the reader and the past. Still, collected documents cannot mirror a past debate, for the accidents of survival preserve key documents and obliterate others. In this case, some Milledgeville public speeches were either never published or have been subsequently lost. Moreover, the editors have omitted one surviving Milledgeville document and highlighted another. In the interests of readability, we have chosen to publish Joseph Brown's revealing public letter of December 7 instead of the governor's fudging Special Message of November 7.

We have also chosen not to publish the massive post-Milledgeville public debate in Georgia, including speeches and/or letters by Henry Jackson, Francis Bartow, Howell Cobb, Linton Stephens, and E. A. Nisbet. Our reason: this book would then be much fattened and little nourished. The confrontation in Milledgeville was conducted at the highest level and it brought forth the essential arguments; rhetoric afterwards echoed the first performances. Moreover, the Milledgeville encounter was seen at the time as its own supreme, inspired moment; we wish to maintain the integrity of the initial showdown. Still, we have included in the Bibliography the location of some excellent post-Milledgeville printed statements, for those who want to read subsequent arguments.

The Milledgevile debate is reprinted verbatim, with clarifications placed in brackets, in the chronological order of the surviving full statements. We have not corrected spelling or grammar, for such errors illuminate statesmen in a rush, hustling to speak and publish before events become unmanageable. That circumstance makes the high quality of the Milledgeville debate all the more striking.

In our footnotes we have restricted ourselves to identification of orators' references. So too, in our Introduction, we have restricted ourselves to portraying the context of the Milledgeville confrontation. Historians will use these debates to defend their own interpretations. But here, the debaters must do the defending.

These choice sources would remain faded and scattered, were it not for those who aided the editors. Craig M. Simpson would like to thank the United States Embassy in Canada and the Social Sciences and Humanities Research Council of Canada, for research and travel support. William W. Freehling would like to thank the endowment of the Thomas B. Lockwood Chair of the State University of New York, Buffalo, for financing the manuscript preparation. We would both like to thank Judith Wozniak, this project's secretary, who somehow produced a clear typescript from blotchy xeroxes, and our research assistant, Richard Keaveny, who expertly checked the text.

New Year's Day, 1992   William W. Freehling
                                          Craig M. Simpson

Contents

1. Thomas R. R. Cobb's Secessionist Speech, Monday
   Evening, November 12   3

2. Robert Toombs's Secessionist Speech, Tuesday
   Evening, November 13   31

3. Alexander H. Stephens's Unionist Speech,
   Wednesday Evening, November 14   51

4. Benjamin H. Hill's Unionist Speech, Thursday
   Evening, November 15   80

5. Herschel V. Johnson's Unionist Public Letter,
   Friday, November 16, from Milledgeville   105

6. Henry L. Benning's Secessionist Speech, Monday
   Evening, November 19   115

7. Joseph E. Brown's Secessionist Public Letter,
   December 7, from Milledgeville   145

   Selected Bibliography   160

SECESSION DEBATED

1

Thomas R. R. Cobb's Secessionist Speech, Monday Evening, November 12

Despite their disagreements politically, the seven Georgia leaders whose polemics are here published had much in common personally. All were in their middle years. Their ages ranged from thirty-seven (Thomas R. R. Cobb and Benjamin H. Hill) to fifty (Robert Toombs). All attended the University of Georgia, except Joseph E. Brown. All were college graduates, again except Brown, who had a Yale law degree. All were Democrats, except Hill, who became a Democrat after the Civil War. All were married and had children, except for that reclusive bachelor, Alexander H. Stephens. All were wealthy Protestant lawyers and slaveholders, with their slaves ranging in number from 13 (Brown) to 300–400 (Toombs). All were, in short, members of the Georgia ruling class.

Only one Georgia ruler shunned the Milledgeville debate. Howell Cobb, United States Secretary of the Treasury, cherished another inner circle: the coterie of National Democrats who had long commanded in Washington. Howell Cobb deplored a potentially secessionist proceeding which might embarrass his pa-

tron, President James Buchanan, before Buchanan gave way to President-elect Abraham Lincoln on March 4, 1861.

With Howell Cobb still clinging to Washington's lame-duck establishment, his younger brother, Thomas R. R. Cobb initiated Georgia's rulers' confrontation. Thomas Cobb never resented Howell Cobb's greater renown, for love and admiration united the brothers. Thomas, like Howell, was a man to be admired. While born and raised a gentleman, Thomas Cobb had not inherited a gentleman's fortune. His father, like Cobbs for generations, had made and lost speculative millions.

Thomas Cobb, wincing at his forebears' gambles, built his (modest) fame and fortune the slow, plodding way. This long-time clerk of the Georgia Supreme Court published the Georgia Reports *in 15 volumes, as well as the* Supreme Court Manual, *the* Digest of Georgia Laws, *and his masterpiece,* An Inquiry into the Law of Negro Slavery. This greatest of southern legal codifiers also prepared an unprecedented (for a southern state) Code of the State of Georgia, *a book Cobb did not live to see. It was published in January, 1863, shortly after he was slain at the Battle of Fredericksburg.*

*Cobb's legal code, like his professional career, featured restraint, control, and a puritanical version of evangelical Christianity. This sometimes lay revivalist wanted government to bar liquor. Cobb also wanted government to force a convicted male seducer to marry the woman or be jailed. "It is a great ... for-*bearance," *Linton Stephens wrote about Cobb's highly intrusive legal code, "that the book does not proscribe rules to govern the chamber maids in the manner of carrying out the piss-pots."*

Yet this advocate of externally imposed control sometimes lacked inner discipline. The court reporter's physique oscillated between thin and pudgy. Other aspects of his daily life also swayed, with his whims of the moment. So volatile a personality inclined towards impulsive disunion. Yet so disciplined a legal clerk preferred a shackled revolution.

Thomas R. R. Cobb advocated controlled rebellion in a

speech at Athens, Georgia, a couple of days before coming to Milledgeville. A listener proclaimed it "the greatest speech I ever heard. . . . Get Mr. Cobb to make the same speech in Milledgeville" and "that dilapidated little village will dissolve the Union forthwith." On November 12, 1860, Cobb gave the following version of his Athens speech, and dilapidated Milledgeville did dissolve into a confrontation over secession.[1]

Gentlemen:

I must return to you my thanks for the courtesy you have extended to me in opening this chamber for my use, and honoring my remarks by your presence. As I do not pretend to be the sagacious politician, or the experienced statesman, (having never, in seventeen years, made a policial speech,) I can attribute this courtesy only to an honest desire on your part to hear what an humble citizen may say at this important crisis in our national affairs. My crude opinions may excite the ridicule of some, and the pity of others, but remember I claim no infallibility for my head, but simply sincerity for my heart. Those of you who know me, can bear witness that I have never in the slightest degree interfered in past political contests, and hence I have no disappointed ambition to satisfy—no personal wrongs to avenge—no party animosity to appease. While you, and others, have been engaged in urging the claims of the respective candidates for the Presidency, who received your suffrages, I have been publishing in Northern newspapers, article after article, arguing, reasoning, urging, persuading, yea,

1. The best biography is William B. McCash, *Thomas R. R. Cobb (1823–1862): The Making of a Southern Nationalist* (Macon, 1983). The Linton Stephens quote is on p. 65. We have transcribed Cobb's speech from *Substance of Remarks Made By Thomas R. R. Cobb, Esq., In The Hall Of The House Of Representatives, Monday Evening, November 12, 1860.* (Atlanta, 1860).

begging our Northern fellow-citizens not to force upon the
South the terrible issue of *Disunion, or Dishonor*. And, candidly, can I say to-night that I would have illuminated my
house with enthusiasm and shoutings, had either one of the
candidates urged in Georgia been elevated to the Presidential
chair.

Surely, then, my friends, you can yield me my claim to
sincerity of heart. And now I admit allegiance to no party. I
propose to serve no party ends. The truth is, there are no parties
in Georgia. Heretofore, we have been divided on questions of
National, not State, policy, and each of us have claimed before
the people, national organizations and a national platform. The
election of last week gave to the winds the claims of us all—
and Democrats and Americans—Bell, Douglas, and Breckinridge men[2]—have all to confess this night, that as national
organizations we are utterly powerless, and our national platforms have been with equal scorn rejected. Why cling, then,
longer to empty names, the names so productive of discord and
hatred? To-night let us bury the hatchet of controversy. The
parties are all dead, let them be buried, and with them let us
bury all the political and personal animosities which they have
engendered, and as brothers, as friends, as Georgia's sons, let
us come and take counsel together, how we shall avenge her
wrongs, promote her prosperity, and preserve her honor.

In times like these, passion should not rule the hour; calm
and dispassionate deliberation should be brought to the con-

---

2. The election of 1860 pitted the Republicans' Abraham Lincoln against
Tennessee's John Bell (candidate of the Constitutional Union Party, sometimes
called the American Party), Illinois's Stephen Douglas (candidate of most
Northern Democrats) and Kentucky's John Breckinridge (candidate of most
Southern Democrats). Douglas carried Missouri; Bell won in Tennessee, Kentucky, and Virginia; Breckinridge swept the other 11 slave states; and Lincoln
won all but three of the northern Electoral College votes. Lincoln ended up
with a clear majority in the Electoral College (59.4%) but a clear minority in
the popular vote (39.9%).

sideration of every question. Even the quick beating pulsations of hearts burning with a sense of injuries should be commanded to "be still," while we survey the past, fully appreciate the present, and peer thoughtfully into the future; avoiding the impetuosity of rashness, and the timidity of fears as well, let us invoke all our human wisdom, and light also from on High, to guide us in our decision. But once decided, let us act, and act like men, men who are determined to do or die.

It is not necessary for me, in addressing this audience, to rehearse the history of those acts which have so often stirred up our hearts to mutiny, and mantled our faces with shame. You know them as well as I—you have felt them as deeply too. Nor shall I presume you are less patriotic, or need my counseling voice to induce you to remember your homes, or your State. The practical issue before us is the triumph of the sectional Black Republican party of the North, and the duty of Georgia in the present emergency. To this I address myself.

Is the election of Lincoln a sufficient ground for the dissolution of the Union?

This may be viewed both as a legal and political question. As a legal question it resolves itself into this. Has he been elected according to the forms and spirit of the Constitution? *Formally,* he has been so elected, when he is so declared by the Congress of the United States. And literally he has been so elected, if the States casting their votes for him are entitled to be counted in the Electoral College; nine of these States, however, casting a combined vote of eighty-five electors, have, by their local legislation, nullified a constitutional act of Congress, and refused to comply with the obligations of the compact when the same are distasteful to the prejudices of their people.[3] As

---

3. Cobb here referred to northern attempts to disrupt enforcement of the Fugitive Slave Law of 1850, either by private action (citizens who passively refused to help hunt down a fugitive slave or actively helped the runaway) or by state action (state governments which in their so-called Personal Liberty

a lawyer, I am prepared to say that parties to such a contract, who have thus violated its provisions when onerous to them, are not entitled to its privileges when demanded by them. And that so long as the "Personal Liberty Bills" disgrace the Statute Books of these States, their electoral votes should not be counted in the Electoral College. But who shall decide upon this question? The Constitution is silent, no provision being made for such a contest. The mode of counting the votes is specified, but no power of decision given to either the Senate or the House, or the General Congress convened. It is an omission in the fundamental law. Who shall decide? The Supreme Court? They have already virtually declared these acts violative of the Constitution, but our opponents and oppressors "spit upon" such decisions. Shall it be decided by force of arms in Washington city? Then civil war must begin there, to end only by the subjugation of one section of the Union. No, my friends, in the absence of any tribunal, the right to decide is one of the "reserved rights" of the States, and Georgia has the privilege of declaring to-day that for herself she decides these votes illegal, and *this election unconstitutional.*

But in another view of this legal question, this man is not chosen as our President. According to the *spirit* of the Constitution, these States have violated its provisions in this election:

First. This Constitution was made for white men—citizens of the United States; this Union was formed by white men, and for the protection and happiness of their race. It is true, that the framers gave to each State the power to declare who should be electors at the ballot-box in each State. But the fair implication was, that this right of suffrage should be given to none but citizens of the United States. Can it be supposed that our fathers intended to allow our national elections to be controlled by men who were not citizens under the National Constitution?

Laws refused to allow state officials to help federal authorities capture fugitive slaves).

Never, never! Yet to elect Abraham Lincoln, the right of suffrage was extended to free negroes in Vermont, Massachusetts, Ohio, New York and other Northern States, although the Supreme Court has declared them not to be citizens of this nation. Yes! Our slaves are first stolen from our midst on underground Railroads,[4] and then voted at Northern ballot-boxes to select rulers for you and me. The memory of our fathers is slandered when this is declared to be according to the Constitution.

But, *secondly*. The spirit of the Constitution has been violated in another particular in this election. Ours is a Republican Government, based upon the democratic principle that the majority have a right to rule. That is an anomalous Government in history or philosophy, which provides for or allows the permanent administration of its powers in the hands of a popular minority. Surely such is not ours. Yet it is true, that counting the unanimous votes of the Southern States and the large minorities in the North against the Black Republicans, a majority amounting to perhaps a million or more votes, have declared against Abraham Lincoln for the next Presidency. Is not this according to the forms of the Constitution? I may be asked. I answer it is. But will my objecting friend answer, is it according to its spirit? I may be told that other Chief Magistrates have been elected by popular minorities. This I admit, but never against such an overwhelming majority, and never by a sectional party based upon the prospect and avowal of a continuation of the same result in every future election. The truth is, that we have lived to see a state of things never contemplated by the framers of the Constitution. At that time we were all slaveholding States—a homogeneous people, having a common origin, common memories—a common cause, common hopes—a common future, a common destiny. The wisdom even of our fathers did not suggest a future when we should

---

4. The loose network of Northerners that sometimes helped fugitive slaves move from hiding place to hiding place.

be a distinct people, having different social organizations, different pursuits, different memories, different hopes, different destinies. And hence, while the Constitution is full of checks to protect the minority from the sudden and excited power of a majority, no provision was suggested for the protection of the majority from the despotic rule of an infuriated, fanatical, sectional minority. The experience of eight years in the Presidential Chair, and the almost more than human wisdom of Washington gave him a glimpse of the fatal omission thus made in the Constitution, and hence we find in that wonderful document—his Farewell Address—a note of solemn warning against such a perversion of the Government, by the formation of sectional parties. What was thus dimly shadowed to his prophetic ken, is the fact of to-day, and will be history to-morrow. Is it not according to the form of the Constitution? I am asked. I answer it is. Tell me it is in accordance with the spirit and frame work?

Third. The preamble to the Constitution of the United States recites the six leading objects for which it was adopted, namely—"To form a more perfect Union, establish justice, ensure domestic tranquility, provide for the common defense, promote the general welfare, and secure the blessings of liberty to ourselves and our posterity." Had I the time, it would be profitable to take each one of these objects and show how fanaticism had perverted this Government from each and every one of the objects of its organization—how "the Union of hearts and hands," which existed prior to the adoption of the Constitution, had given way to sectional jealousies and mutual hatred—how justice had been denied under the quibbles of executive traitors, outraged both on the bench and in the jury-box—how the common defence had been construed into local advantage, and the general welfare been found in the fleecing of our producers for the fattening of their manufacturers. But these results are not specially attributable to the event we now consider—the election of Lincoln—and hence, I call your attention only to two of these objects—the ensuring of domestic tranquility, and the securing of the blessings of liberty. Recur with me to the parting moment when you left your firesides, to attend upon your public duties at the Capitol. Remember the trembling hand of a loved wife, as she whispered her fears from the incendiary and the assassin. Recall the look of indefinable dread with which the little daughter inquired when your returning footsteps should be heard. And if there be manhood in you, tell me if this is the domestic tranquility which this "glorious Union" has achieved. Notice the anxious look when the travelling pedlar lingers too long in conversation at the door with the servant who turns the bolt—the watchful gaze when the slave tarries long with the wandering artist who professes merely to furnish him with a picture—the suspicion aroused by a Northern man conversing in private with the most faithful of your negroes, and tell me if peace and tranquility are the heritage which this Union has brought to your firesides. Take up your daily papers, and see reports of insurrections in every direction. Hear the telegram read which announces another John Brown raid.[5] Travel on your Railroads and hear, as I did this day, that within seven miles of this Capitol, a gang of slaves have revolted from their labor, declaring themselves free by virtue of Lincoln's election, and say if such fruits as these grow on the good tree of domestic tranquility. Mark me, my friends, I have no fear of any servile insurrection which shall threaten our political existence. Our slaves are the most happy and contented, best fed and best clothed and best paid laboring population in the world, and I would add, also, the *most faithful* and least feared. But a discontented few here and there, will become the incendiary or the poisoner, when insti-

5. The swiftly defeated invasion of Massachusetts' John Brown, along with a handful of Yankees, on Harpers Ferry Arsenal in Virginia in 1859. Brown sought to undermine the slavocracy from within, maybe even to inspire a slave revolt.

gated by the unscrupulous emissaries of Northern Abolitionists, and you and I cannot say but that your home or your
family may be the first to greet your returning footsteps in
ashes or in death.—What has given impulse to these fears, and
aid and comfort to those outbreaks now, but the success of the
Black Republicans—the election of Abraham Lincoln!

I need hardly consume your time in adverting to the clause
as to "securing the blessings of liberty to ourselves and our
posterity." What liberty have we secured by the Constitution
of the United States? Our personal liberty is protected by the
broad aegis of Georgia's sovereignty. To her we never appealed
in vain. What liberty does the Union give us? The glorious
liberty of being robbed of our property, threatened in our lives,
abused and villified in our reputation on every forum from the
grog-shop to the Halls of Congress, libelled in every vile newspaper, and in every town meeting, deprived of all voice in the
election of our Chief Magistracy, bound to the car of a fiendish
fanaticism, which is daily curtailing every vestige of our privileges, and by art and cunning, under the forms of the Constitution, binding us in a vassalage more base and hopeless than
that of the Siberian serf. This is "glorious" liberty secured by
a "glorious Union." And the election of Lincoln by a purely
sectional vote, and upon a platform of avowed hostility to our
rights and our liberty, is the cap-stone—nay, the last *magna
carta*—securing to us these wonderful privileges. Is not all this
according to the forms of the Constitution? I am asked. I answer
it is. But tell me, Union-loving friends, is this its spirit?

Fourth. Equality among the States is the fundamental idea
of the American Union. Protection to the life, liberty and property of the citizen is the corner-stone and only end of Government in the American mind. Look to the party whose triumph
is to be consummated in the inauguration of Lincoln—The exclusive enjoyment of all the common territory of the Union, is
their watchword and party cry. The exclusion of half the States
of the Union has been decreed, and we are called upon to record

the *fiat*. Will you do it, men of Georgia? Are you so craven so soon?

But protection—whence comes it to us? Dare you to follow your fugitive into a Northern State to arrest him? The assassin strikes you down, and no law avenges your blood; your property is stolen every day, and the very attempt to recover it subjects you to the insults of the North, and the smile of derision at your folly, at home. A province of Great Britain[6] now covers, with the protection of her flag, millions of dollars of your property and mine. Let a fishing smack from New Bedford be taken into a Canadian port, and the cry of British insolence resounds through the land. A demand for redress is made, and the threat goes with it to let loose the dogs of war! And yet no Administration of the Government has ever yet been bold enough even to ask for the restitution of our property.—Nay, more, so cowed have we become that no Representative from the South has ever even complained of the wrong. But there is something more valuable than property, more dear than life. It is the good name a father bequeathed us, and the inheritance we hold dearest, to descend to our children. How is it protected? On the floor of Congress we are taunted with our weakness and our cowardice, and all the crimes of the calendar—murder, arson, rape, robbery—all compare not in enormity, we are told by our own rulers and law-makers, with that greatest of all sins, that most horrible of all crimes, the holding of slaves! Where, then, is our protection, and for what owe we allegiance to this Government? Georgia extends her sovereign arm over us, and our lives, our property, our liberty and our reputation are safe under her protection. Loyalty and fidelity have reason for their growth and food for their sustenance when we turn to this good old Commonwealth. But when we look to this Union—oh, tell me—why owe we allegiance to it? Long have I loved it. Blindly

6. Canada.

have I worshipped it. I bade selfishness avaunt, when my heart
turned toward the Government of my fathers. I remembered
only that it came from the minds and hearts of Washington,
and Henry, and Adams, and Pinckney, and Madison, and Rut-
ledge. I saw the glories of Bunker Hill, and Monmouth, and
Saratoga, and Yorktown, clustering around it.—I recalled the
story of her struggles as an aged ancestor who bled in her cause
recounted it to infant ears around the winter's fire. I remembered a father's instructions, and had witnessed a father's devotion, and I fell down and worshipped at a shrine where he
worshipped before me, and dared not to inquire into the cause
of my devotion. But when the cruel hand of Northern aggression aroused me from my worship, when it tore away the thin
veil which covered the idol before me, I could but weep as the
heartstrings were snapped from their attachment, though I
woke to discover that I had been bowing before a veiled prophet
of Mokannah,[7] whose deformity and ugliness disgusted while
they pained me!

Ten years ago, some of you, wiser than I was, warned me
of my delusion, but I clung to my hope, when to you there was
none, and to-night I give you the meed of praise for a clearer
foresight, and a less blind devotion. But this very fact makes
me charitable to them who may still bow at the shrine of the
Union. It is almost cruel to dispel their illusion, but I cannot
help feeling that the time must come, and come quickly, when
the veiled prophet shall say to them as he has said to me—

"Ye would be fools, and fools ye are."

Time warns me that I cannot pursue this inquiry farther. As

7. Presumably the Brahman king, Mukanna, responsible for introducing
Hinduism into a portion of the Indian subcontinent during the third century
A.D.

a legal question, I am compelled to decide that the election of Lincoln is in violation of the spirit of the Constitution of the United States. And am I told this spirit is too indefinite and shadowy a substance to be made the basis of resistance? And can there be a Georgian who will never resist so long as the form and letter of the Constitution is not broken? Let us inquire. The inter-State Slave Trade is within the letter of the Constitution. Should Congress abolish it will my objector submit? The amendment of the Constitution itself is within the letter of that instrument. If it is so amended in accordance with its letter as to carry out Lincoln's announcement that the States must be all free, will my objector submit? Why not? Because these are violative of its spirit. Truly, my friends, in the words of inspiration, "the letter killeth, but the spirit giveth life." To the spirit then we must look, and a violation of that spirit renders this election unconstitutional.

I come now to consider this question in its *political* light, and it rises in importance much above the mere legal question.

I must confess that the mere election of a candidate to the Presidency, in a manner legally unconstitutional, does not in my judgment justify necessarily a dissolution of the Union. The wise man and the statesman, to say nothing of the patriot, will always weigh well whether "it is better to bear the ills we have than fly to others that we know not of." And, hence, arises the *political* question, does this election justify and require a disruption of the ties which bind us to the Union? As much as I would dislike the triumph of a purely sectional candidate upon a purely sectional platform, I am free to say I should hesitate even then to risk the consequences of a dissolution, provided that sectional platform *was upon issues not vital in themselves, or were temporary in their nature.* Such, would I conceive to be protective tariffs and homestead bills—the acquisition of territory—peace or war with foreign powers. And if the election of Lincoln, unconstitutional though it may be, was upon a temporary issue, or a question not vital in importance, I should hesitate to declare it ground for Disunion. But my countrymen, I cannot so view the triumph of Black Republicanism. It is a question vital in itself, and by no means, of a temporary character. To see it in its breadth and enormity, to see its dangerous proportions and its threatening aspects, it becomes necessary for us to go back a little in history, and to trace the slavery agitation as connected with our Government. Shortly after its organization, we find a petition from the Quakers of Philadelphia, asking the abolition of slavery. We see that petition treated by an unanimous Congress as the mere ebullition of religious fanaticism, and as it is laid on the table, we smile at the folly of the broadbrim followers of Fox.[8] In a few years we find petitions accumulating from other Sects and Societies, until, finally, by an overwhelming majority, we find the House of Representatives refusing longer to listen to their fanatical ravings, and as the 21st Rule[9] is adopted, we fondly dreamed that the cockatrice's egg would never be hatched. In a few years we find the floor of Congress desecrated by the ravings of Giddings[10] and other abolitionists, and at the same time, in the Presidential contest, an abolition candidate is presented to the people of the North.[11] But the Abolitionists in Congress are hissed at their ravings, and the miserable handful at the ballot-box only manifested their weakness, and we rested secure in our confidence in the protection of the Constitution.

But a few years more found the miserable demagogues and political leaders of the North, in their party excitement, bidding for this Abolition vote. Without real sympathy for the move-

8. George Fox, 1624–91, founder of the English Society of Friends.

9. The most extreme of the "Gag Rules" passed in Congress, 1836–44. These "Gag Rules" outlawed congressional discussion of any petition concerning slavery.

10. Joshua R. Giddings, for twenty years an antislavery congressman from Ohio.

11. The Liberty Party, which in 1840 and 1844 ran James Birney as a third party antislavery candidate for the presidency.

ment, we find them vieing with each other in pretended zeal, until shortly we find the 21st Rule falling as a sacrifice before the demands of the fanatics.[12] We find the parties in power more and more undecided in denouncing the treason, until finally the great Whig party fell, demoralized, and at the North very much Abolitionized.[13] We find church organizations, and great benevolent institutions, one after another, sundered and divided by the demon, which, once aroused, there was no power to allay.[14] We find reason and argument unheeded, the obligations of oaths and compacts disregarded, the very religion of God desecrated, His Bible denounced, His churches and pulpits polluted, and His children excluded from the communion table of their Master. And then, for the first time, we awake to the great fact that our lives and liberty are in jeopardy unless great exertions for our safety are made. In the meantime, our slaves are stolen, the old remedies are proved useless, new provisions are demanded. The Post Offices become the vehicles of spreading insurrection, and new restrictions are required. Greater demands are made in Congress, and States rejected from the Union because Slavery is recognized by their Constitutions.[15] Finally, the slave trade in the District of Columbia is attacked, and the inter-State slave trade. The Wilmot proviso is placed on all territory,[16] and the South aroused to her danger, demands

12. The last gag rule was repealed in December, 1844.

13. The Whig Party split apart after the Kansas-Nebraska Act of 1854, for its northern wing had become too anti-southern to be acceptable in the Deep South.

14. In 1844–45, both the Baptist and Methodist national churches split into northern and southern wings.

15. Cobb to the contrary, no state was rejected solely because it had slavery. But the admission of Missouri, 1819–21, and Texas, 1843–45, were opposed and delayed for that reason. Kansas, when applying for admission as a slave state, was rejected in 1858, but arguably more because Congress believed that a majority of Kansans opposed slavery than because the Kansas Lecompton Constitution upheld the institution.

16. The Wilmot Proviso, proposed by Congressman David Wilmot of Penn-

security and peace. We all remember the great Compromise
measures of 1850.[17] They were declared a *finality,* and the syren
song of peace was sung in our ears. Some of us believed it, and
we once more laid down in ease. Soon, however, a new question
is raised, the monster shows himself again in the Halls of Congress, and once more we hear that the Union is saved and peace
restored by the provisions of the Kansas-Nebraska Act.[18] The
other events are known to you. This Black Republican party
is formed; Fremont is its candidate;[19] let us crush it now, and
the Slavery issue is dead forever. Such was the song. Great
exertions are made. Fremont is defeated, and we hope on for
peace. There seems to be a lull in the storm. One of Georgia's
distinguished sons voluntarily terminates his long public car-
reer [sic], and as he bids farewell to his constituents, he informs
us in a public address (honestly, I have no doubt), that the
battle is over, the victory won, that he lays off his armor be-

---

sylvania in 1846, during the Mexican War, sought to bar slavery in all territories gained from the Mexican War. Cobb to the contrary, the Proviso never
became law, although the North-controlled House of Representatives several
times passed the ban on territorial slavery. Lincoln in 1860 campaigned to
implement a Wilmot-Proviso-like ban on slavery in all national territories,
which was a critical reason why secessionists such as Cobb refused to "submit"
to "Black Republican" rule.

17. The congressional settlement of the crisis of 1850, which included the
admission of free California as a state, passage of a new fugitive slave law,
no decision on whether slavery should be abolished or protected in Mexican
Cession territories, the outlawing of auctions for selling slaves in Washington,
D.C., and United States assumption of Texas state debts in return for Texas's
compromise on its state boundaries.

18. The act passed by Congress in 1854 which repealed the Missouri
Compromise congressional ban—passed in 1820—on slavery in Kansas and
Nebraska territories. The decision on slavery's status was left to the settlers
in the two territories, leading to a race between Northerners and Southerners
to the area—and also leading to bloodshed in Bleeding Kansas.

19. John C. Frémont, candidate of the Republican Party in 1856. Frémont
swept the North except for New Jersey, Illinois, Indiana, California, and
Pennsylvania.

cause there is no other foe to meet, and he shows to our willing ears what great things had been done for us, "whereof we were glad."[20] But hardly had he reached his quiet home, ere the territory of Virginia is invaded by a lawless band under John Brown, and to-day you find him with his armor again buckled on, to resave the Union once more—to re-deliver us from the fanatical devil. And now, after four years of argument and persuasion, and entreaty and remonstrance and warning, to-night, my friends, we find this demon, master of our strongholds, this party, so long to be destroyed, more rampant and more triumphant than ever—with almost fabulous majorities in every Northern State—placing in the Executive Chair one of the most objectionable and fanatical of its leaders. Are we blind, that this retrospect shall teach us no lesson? Read upon the banners of this army, and see what are its objects and aims: *"No more Slave States;" "The Repeal of the Fugitive Slave Law;" "Relief from the Slave Power;" "The Irrepressible Conflict;" "No League with Hell."* Look at its leaders, and see the heroes who deify John Brown; the mad preachers, like Cheever and Beecher; the Fourierites, led by Greely; the Sewards, and Sumners, and Hales, and Fred Douglas [sic].[21] Look at its cohorts, and see their mottled ranks—free negroes and boot-blacks, coachmen and domestics, infidels and free-lovers, spiritual rappers and every other shade of mania and folly. Search in vain among them all, for one gentleman like Everett, one sound

20. Alexander Stephens, who had temporarily retired from politics in 1859.

21. Cobb here referred to some of the most notorious Republican opponents of the South: the Rev. George B. Cheever and the Rev. Henry Ward Beecher; the newspaper editor Horace Greeley of the *New York Tribune,* who sometimes espoused the socialist principles of the French reformer, Charles Fourier; United States Senators William H. Seward of New York and Charles Sumner of Massachusetts; John P. Hale of New Hampshire, the Free Soil candidate for the presidency in 1852; and Frederick Douglass, the black fugitive slave, autobiographer, and abolitionist orator/editor.

conservative like Fillmore, one bold statesman like Cushing or O'Connor, one noble patriot like Buchanan, one daring leader like Douglas.[22] Scan closely all its long lists of speakers or voters as far as we can see them, and where is the man you would ask into your table, or with whose arm you would walk through your streets. *And yet these are our rulers.* To them we are called to submit. Let me rather have a king, for I can respect him; or an emperor, for I may cajole him; or an aristocracy, for they will not envy, and dare not hate me. Nay, let me die before I shall bow before such fanatics as these.

The question, then, is vital. Is it temporary? The history of its insignificant rise and rapid progress—the little cloud, no bigger than a man's hand, which has now overspread the whole Heavens—the thunders which we hear too distinctly to be misunderstood—the insolence which even the prospect of power has given to craven cowards—that already they taunt us with timidity and threaten us with chastisement—aye, a hundred indications too plain to be mistaken, say to everything but stolid ignorance or blind fatuity, that this is but "the beginning of the end." My friends, history and philosophy would have informed us years ago of the same truth, had we listened to their teachings. Fanaticism is madness, is insanity. It has a zeal laudable in its earnestness, admirable in its honesty. Its error is in the false foundation on which it builds. Its danger lies in the depth of its convictions, which will not allow it to attend to reason, but makes it as "the deaf adder which will not listen to the charmers, charming never so wisely." Its fountain lies deep in the human heart. Its bonds are interwoven with many of the noblest principles of our nature. Hence, it ignores consequences, it overrides obstacles, it ruthlessly sun-

22. Cobb here referred to Edward Everett and Caleb Cushing of Massachusetts, ex-President (1850–53) Millard Fillmore, President James Buchanan, Illinois Senator Stephen A. Douglas, and Charles O'Conor, a New York City lawyer with proslavery sympathies.

ders the dearest ties of the heart, it takes affection from the lover, yea, it steels the mother against her own offspring, the creature against his God. We call it blind, because it cannot see; we call it deaf, because it cannot hear; we call it foolish, because it cannot reason; we call it cruel, because it cannot feel. By what channel, then, can you reach its citadel? Firmly planted therein, with every avenue closed to ingress, and yet every door of evil influence open to the bitter issues which flow without, the deluded victim glories in his own shame, and scatters ruin and destruction, in the mad dream that he is doing God's service. Such is the teaching of philosophy, and history, her handmaid, confirms its truth. The bloody minds of those who, with sinful hands, murdered the Lord of Glory, were never sated until the Roman legions sacked the city of David, and the Eagle of Rome floated over the ruins of the Temple.[23] The fires of Smithfield never ceased to burn until the maiden Queen, with her strong arm and stronger will, sealed in the blood of Mary, the covenant of peace to the Church.[24] The wheel of the Juggernaut never failed to crush the bones of infatuated victims, until the shaggy main [sic] of the British Lion was drenched in the blood of Oriental imbecility.[25] The bloody Crescent of the false prophet never ceased to behold the gory victims which Islam claimed, until on many a battle-field the redemption in blood came to rescue the children of Faith.[26] The Ganges bore in its turbid waters the innocent victims of the delusion

23. In 71 A.D. a Roman army under Emperor Titus sacked Jerusalem and destroyed the Temple.

24. More than two hundred Protestants were burned at the stake in Smithfield on authority of Queen Mary of England, prior to her death in 1558. Mary's sister Elizabeth succeeded her on the throne.

25. The Juggernaut was a Hindu idol annually dragged through worshipful cities on a huge chariot. Fanatics threw themselves under the wheels, hoping that they would go to paradise. Juggernaut, when used figuratively, stands for an institution or nation for which people blindly sacrifice themselves.

26. The followers of Muhammad had never been reticent about shedding their blood, particularly in *jihads,* or holy wars, waged on behalf of Islam.

of mothers, until Britain assumed the position which God held
to Abraham on the Mount, and staying the murderous arms,
bade the well-spring of a mother's love once more to gush from
a mother's heart.[27] Why should I continue the review? All history speaks but one voice. Tell me when and where the craving
appetite of fanaticism was ever gorged with victims; when and
where its bloody hands were ever stayed by the consciousness
of satiety; when and where its deaf ears ever listened to reason,
or argument, or persuasion, or selfishness; when and where it
ever died from fatigue, or yielded except in blood. And when
you have done this, you may then convince me that this is a
temporary triumph, and bid me to hope on. Till you do this, I
must listen to the teachings of reason, philosophy and history,
and believe that Lincoln and Seward spoke the truth when
they said, this contest is never ended until all these States are
either free or slave.[28]

Mark me, my friends! The only tie which binds together
this party at the North is the Slavery issue. Bank and anti-
Bank, Protection and Free Trade, Old Whig and Old Democrat,
have all come together. The old issues are ignored, forgotten.
Abolitionism and Agrarianism are the only specialities in their
platform. This Aaron's rod[29] has swallowed up all the others,
and upon it alone has the battle been fought and the victory
won. And no man and no party can make terms or obtain

27. Female infanticide persisted, particularly in the central and western
portions of the Indian subcontinent, until the later years of the nineteenth
century, despite British and local efforts to suppress it.

28. Cobb here referred to notorious prophecies of Illinois's Lincoln and
New York's Seward, where they talked of "a House Divided that cannot Stand"
(Lincoln) and an "Irrepressible Conflict" (Seward). Actually, neither of these
"Black Republicans" were as consistently radical as these momentary excla-
mations seem to imply.

29. Aaron, Moses's younger brother, whose rod budded with the fruit of
almonds when left overnight in the tabernacle. All the other elders' rods remained but rods, showing that Aaron and his family alone were divinely
appointed as high priests.

quarter from these fanatics, except by bowing down and worshipping this Moloch.[30] Even in this election, have not the Southern parties offered candidates on every shade of opinion, to this Northern horde, and have they not all been rejected with scorn? Did not Bell and Douglas and Breckinridge, one or the other, agree with them on every question except Slavery? Why were they rejected? Herculean efforts have been made. Argument and eloquence have been offered lavishly, and money almost as lavishly, to bid off and buy up this motley crew. Scorn, contempt, insolence and contumely have been the only answer we have received. Can any man shut his eyes and still cry the syren song, "Hope on? Hope on?"

We have seen, then, that this election is *legally* unconstitutional, and that *politically* the issue on which it is unconstitutional is both *vital* in its importance and *permanent* in its effects. What, then, is our remedy? Shall it be the boy's redress of recrimination? the bully's redress of braggadocio or boasting? or the manly freeman's redress of Independence? This is a most solemn question, and no man should rashly advise his countrymen at such a time. For myself, for months, nay years, I have forseen this coming cloud. I have given it all the study of which my mind is possessed. I have called my heart into the council and listened to its beatings. Nay, more, my friends. I fear not to say I have gone to the God I worship, and begged Him to advise me. On the night of the 6th of November,[31] I called my wife and little ones together around my family altar, and together we prayed to God to stay the wrath of our oppressors, and preserve the Union of our fathers. The rising sun of the seventh of November found me on my knees, begging the same kind Father to make that wrath to praise Him, and the remainder of wrath to restrain. I believe that the hearts of

30. In the Old Testament, a deity worshipped by the Ammonites, to whom children were sacrificed by fire.
31. The night of Lincoln's election.

men are in His hands, and when the telegraph announced to
me that the voice of the North proclaimed at the ballot-box
that I should be a slave, I heard in the same sound, the voice
of my God speaking through His Providence, and saying to his
child, "Be free! Be free!"

Marvel not then that I say my voice is for *immediate, unconditional secession.*

The suggestion for delay comes from various quarters.
Good men, and true men, hesitate as to the time. Their counsel
deserves attention. Their very doubts are entitled to consideration. Let me then trespass a little longer on your time, to
answer the question, shall we delay?

What are their hopes, and on what are they based? I have
shown that we cannot expect this fanatical spirit to die, or be
appeased. What then shall we look for? From one, I hear the
suggestion that perhaps Lincoln may betray his party, and like
Fillmore prove to be a conservative. Oh, shame! shame! shame!
Is it come to this, that the only hope of Georgia is in the treason
of an abolitionist? False to his friends, can you trust him?—
False to his friends, can you reward him? Can even the con-
solations of conscience be held out as an inducement to a perjured traitor? But suppose he did prove traitor, what then?
Would not these blood-hounds only seek in Seward, or Sumner,
or Hale, a less scrupulous and more faithful servant? And would
not the very mortification of disappointment only whet more
keenly their appetite for blood? From another, I hear the suggestion that the Senate can refuse to ratify his appointments,
and thus he will be without a cabinet, and without an administration. What is this my friends but revolution and anarchy?
We destroy one Government without providing another. And
more, and worse, we require our Senators to disregard their
oaths to the Constitution, and while within the temple to pull
down its pillars. True, like Sampson [sic], they may destroy
the Philistines, but like Sampson [sic], too, we shall share their

fate.[32] Better far, peacably [sic] to withdraw, and let their God smile on them with prosperity, if He wills it, while our God shall bless us, who doing no man harm, seek only to worship in our own holy hill.

From another, I hear that we have both Houses of Congress, and hence, Lincoln is powerless. How blindly mistaken! The Executive branch of the Government alone can protect us. The President only can call out the Army and Navy. The President only can appoint Commissioners, and Marshals, and Judges, to execute the Fugitive Slave Law. The President only can protect us from armed invasions and secret incendiaries. I admit that it is so feeble that we can hope but little from it, even with a friend as President—with a foe, what can we hope? But I am told, suppose Lincoln, in his inaugural, pledges himself to carry out these laws. I would not believe him on his oath. Let them who can trust a Black Republican Abolitionist, hug to their bosom the fatal delusion that we can hope for sweet waters from such a poisoned fountain. Moreover, why wait for two years when at their close we hope for nothing? Will our hearts become braver by submitting to this rule? Will our arms become stronger by the paralysis of shame? Will our people be more unanimous when party spirit has enchained them by its bonds? The restive bullock chafes when the tender skin first feels the heavy yoke, but a few days hardens the neck, and the sober, patient ox receives uncomplainingly the lash and the goad as well as the yoke. Two years of shame may crush out mountains of patriotism. No man dares say now I love this Union for its blessings. To-day, if the question was

32. Samson, deliverer of Israel, conquered the Philistines. They then conquered him by bribing his lover, Delilah, to cut off the source of his strength: his hair. When Samson's hair grew back, he tore down the pillars which supported the temple where he was on display, killing himself and 3000 of his captors.

submitted to Georgia independent—shall we go into this Union? ten voters could not be found who would choose such a league with death. Why should ten be found who would choose to continue this league? Ah! the cry of "Union" has been a tower of strength, and I fear that some, yes, many, fearing the effect on the people, will still stand by the watchword after the citadel is in ashes. But, gentlemen, such leaders do injustice to our people. They were loyal to their Government while it was *their* Government. When it became the mere tool of their enemies, they will spurn it with a unanimity which will overwhelm their slanderers.

None of these arguments or suggestions carry conviction to my mind. While hope of better things lived, I could be patient and hope on; but when hope died, darkness came, and the only gleam of light in the dark horizon which meets my eye, is from Georgia's star—independent—and if necessary—alone. But we shall not be alone. Our sister on the East[33] holds out imploring arms to welcome us in our march. Our daughters on the West (Alabama and Mississippi) wait only for their mother to speak. Our neighbor on the South,[34] to whom just now we are generously yielding a portion of our territory, begs for our counsel and our lead. Georgia, Empire State as she is and deserves to be, must be no laggard in the race. The head of the column is her birthright and her due. To the column's head let us march!

My friends, there is danger in delay. The North, flushed with victory, construes and will construe every indication of hesitancy into a dastardly fear—every voice for delay into the quakings of cowardice. The stern, unyielding look of the brave man makes the snarling cur sneak back to his kennel, but let the cheek blench before the foe, and the lip quiver, and the knees shake, and do you wonder that when you do stand your ground, the miserable cur is biting at your heels? Delay, there-

33. South Carolina.
34. Florida.

fore, invites aggression and destroys all confidence in our courage. Let Georgia speak now, and a Northern Regiment will never cross the border line. Let Georgia delay, and they will make scourges to whip the cowards to obedience. Delay is dangerous, because now, we have at the North a respectable body of men who sympathize with us in our oppression, and will not aid the oppressor. They are melting away like frost-work before the burning zeal of this fanatical sun, and ere long their own thinned ranks, and their inevitable contempt for our timidity will render them powerless as a barrier to Northern aggression. Delay is dangerous, because now the Army and Navy are in the hands of an Administration that recognizes our right to withdraw. On the fourth day of March next, the powerful arm of the Executive will be wielded by a foe as unrelenting as he is cruel. Delay is dangerous, because it demoralizes our position—takes away from our cause its justice in the eyes of the world—enervates the arms that are now ready to rise in our defence, and chills the hearts that are now burning with patriotic zeal. Delay is dangerous, because it keeps open our territory to the emissaries of the North—teaches us to weigh our honor in the selfish scales of interest, and drives back to die, the warm out-gushing feelings of wounded hearts.

Shall I be told that the country is prosperous, that the crops are good, that money is plenty, and the people feel not the iron heel of the oppressor? I will not answer by predicting a financial crisis, and ruin, and distress, and the crash of hard-times upon us. I will not allude to the difficulties already felt in financial circles, and the distrust, which like the Barometer, ever indicates the coming storm. No, I have more confidence than you, my objector, in the people's wisdom. Behold on yonder ocean the leaking vessel.—See the indications of her fate in the gradual, slow but sure rising of the water on her bows. On the upper, aye, *the upper* deck, behold the gay party basking in the warm sunshine and rejoicing in the gentle breeze. Do you tell me, when I warn them of their danger, and point them to the approaching billows, they will answer that they cannot move, because the sunlight of Heaven is bright around them and the zephyr fans sweetly their wearied limbs? No, never. They will weigh my evidence, they will examine into the hold, they will act as wise men before they are engulphed in the sea. Fear not the people! The coward may quake—a few luxuriating in ease may shut their eyes to their danger—many may be deceived, but the great heart of this great people will respond to the voice of reason, to the call of patriotism.

Shall I be told to wait for an *overt* act? What act do you expect? What act will be overt? Are not the nullifying Personal Liberty Bills of nine States, *overt?* Are not the daily thefts of our negroes by underground Railroads, *overt?* Are not the national thefts of our national territory, *overt?* Was not the John Brown raid, invading the territory of the South, *overt?* Is not the election of these sectional candidates over a broken Constitution, *overt?* What is the overt act you wish? Does any man expect these wily, crafty lyers-in-wait, to declare the Constitution a nullity—or to march with bold tread over its fragments? They can bind us hand and foot, and sell us into Slavery, and never commit such an overt act, and every Statesman in the country can explain to you the process. Shall I be told that the present is an abstraction, and not a practical issue? The man that urges that, would be hard to convince that the abolition of Slavery in the District of Columbia is not an abstraction, because there are very few slaves there. Would he not ask you, will you destroy this "glorious Union" for that small patch of ground? Is not the repeal of the Fugitive Slave Law an abstraction, because we all know that even now it is almost a dead letter? And would not the objector again sing paeans to this Union? The Wilmot Proviso is an abstraction, because climate and the laws of God have forbidden the negro to leave the warm sun of the South. Oh! where is the overt act for which you are asked to delay? I can imagine nothing else than the assassin's knife at your throat, and the incendiary's torch under your dwelling. My friends, delay is dangerous, for ere long you will be imprisoned by walls of free States all around you. Your increasing slaves will drive out the only race that can move— the whites—and the masters who still cling to their father's graves, will, like the scorpion in a ring of fire, but sting themselves to die. This is your destiny *in the Union. Out of it,* you have a glorious soil—immense natural resources—cotton, the great peace-maker of the world—the best social and political organizations on earth—a people firm, free and independent— the smile of the God we worship illumining our path, and the voice of that God saying, "Occupy till I come."

But the last and most potent argument to my mind in favor of immediate action, is, that by it alone can we preserve peace. I think I have shown that we have no danger to fear from servile insurrection, nor from Northern bayonets. Whence, then, is the danger? At home, among ourselves, with Georgia as the theatre, and our brethren as the victims. Suppose we are equally divided. A small majority will decide the question? As good citizens we ought to submit. I should surely so counsel all my fellow citizens. But you know, and I know, that there are zealous, warm spirits who would rather grace a traitor's gallows than to wear the badge of a slave. Collisions between them and the General Government are almost inevitable. What then? Will this arm be raised to strike them down? Never, no, never! Will you stand by and see them gibbeted on Federal bayonets, or sentenced by Federal Courts? I have spoken for myself; answer now for yourselves. When the dogs of war first lap the blood of freemen, what will be the consequences. I think I see in the future a gory head rise above our horizon. Its name is Civil War. Already I can see the prints of his bloody fingers upon our lintels and door-posts. The vision sickens me already, and I turn your view away. Oh! Georgians, avert from your State this bloody scourge. Surely your love of Union is not so great but that you can offer it on the altar of fraternal peace. Come then, legislators, selected as you are to represent the wisdom and intelligence of Georgia; wait not till the grog-shops and cross-roads shall send up a discordant voice from a divided people, but act as leaders, in guiding and forming public opinion. Speak no uncertain words, but let your united voice go forth to be resounded from every mountain top and echoed from every gaping valley; let it be written in the rainbow which spans our Falls, and read in the crest of every wave upon our ocean shores, until it shall put a tongue in every bleeding wound of Georgia's mangled honor which shall cry to Heaven for "Liberty or Death!"

2

Robert Toombs's Secessionist Speech, Tuesday Evening, November 13

If Thomas R. R. Cobb, the impulsive revolutionary, longed for control, Robert Toombs never felt a restraint he enjoyed. Antebellum Georgians loved this irrepressible charmer. No politician in the state was so popular. No courtroom lawyer was in such demand. Few planters were so rich. Toombs had represented Georgia in Congress since 1846 and in the United States Senate since 1851. Through it all, instead of seeking to discipline himself and others, in T. R. R. Cobb's manner, Toombs grew more portly, more fond of strong drink, more erratic. He exemplified the flamboyant cavalier, charging hither and yon in defense of his honor.

After delivering the following secessionist speech, Toombs would become the state's most confusing leader. In early December, 1860, he would advocate one last attempt at compromise. Two weeks later, he would urge uncompromising secession. Georgia's unsteady hero would then slide towards oblivion. His left arm would be shattered on the Antietam battlefield. His political power would be shattered in a losing campaign for the

Confederate Senate. His fortune would be shattered by northern
victory. He would spend 1865–67 fleeing from New Orleans to
Havana to London, lest Northerners jail him. When he finally
arrived back in his beloved Georgia, he would sink into drunk-
enness and decrepitude.

But back on November 13, 1860, in Milledgeville, Georgia's
favorite antebellum knight had re-earned his admirers' adu-
lation. His speech did not feature invincible logic or stunning
abstraction. Robert Toombs instead exuded something perhaps
more important: the emotional fury of the secessionist.[1]

GENTLEMEN OF THE GENERAL ASSEMBLY: I very
much regret, in appearing before you at your request, to address
you on the present state of the country, and the prospect before
us, that I can bring you no good tidings. The stern, steady march
of events has brought us in conflict with our non-slaveholding
confederates upon the fundamental principles of our compact
of Union. We have not sought this conflict; we have sought too
long to avoid it; our forbearance has been construed into weakness, our magnanimity into fear, until the vindication of our
manhood, as well as the defence of our rights, is required at

---

1. The latest biography is William Y. Thompson, *Robert Toombs of Georgia* (Baton Rouge, 1966). We have transcribed Toombs's speech from Frank
Moore, ed., *The Rebellion Record: A Diary of American Events* (11 vol.; New
York, 1861–63; 1864–68), Supplement to Vol. 1, pp. 362–68. The Rare Book
Room of the Library of Congress holds a pamphlet copy of the speech. Minor
textual differences distinguish it from the version reprinted here. Since it
proved impossible to identify Toombs's original text, the editors have decided
to republish Moore's previously more accessible version. Yet another text also
exists, which includes even less important variations, entitled *Speech of Hon.
Robert Toombs, on the Crisis, Delivered Before the Georgia Legislature*. Published in Washington by Lemuel Towers, it was *erroneously dated* December
7, 1860.

our hands. The door of conciliation and compromise is finally closed by our adversaries, and it remains only to us to meet the conflict with the dignity and firmness of men worthy of freedom. We need no declaration of independence. Above eighty-four years ago our fathers won that by the sword from Great Britian, and above seventy years ago Georgia, with the twelve other confederates, as free, sovereign, and independent States, having perfect governments already in existence, for purposes and objects clearly expressed, and with powers clearly defined, erected a common agent for the attainment of these purposes by the exercise of those powers, and called this agent the United States of America.

The basis, the corner-stone of this Government, was the perfect equality of the free, sovereign, and independent States which made it. They were unequal in population, wealth, and territorial extent—they had great diversities of interests, pursuits, institutions, and laws; but they had common interests, mainly exterior, which they proposed to protect by this common agent—a constitutional united government—without in any degree subjecting their inequalities and diversities to Federal control or action. Peace and commerce with foreign nations could be more effectually and cheaply cultivated by a common agent; therefore they gave the Federal Government the sole management of our relations with foreign governments. The conflicts of interests and the passions of rulers and people bring wars—their effectual prosecution and the common defence could be more certainly and cheaply attained by putting the power of each under the control of a common agent; hence the power of peace and war was given to the Government. These powers made armies, navies, and foreign agents necessary— these could only be maintained by a common treasury. Besides, we had a large debt, contracted at home and abroad in our War of Independence; therefore the great power of taxation was conferred upon this Government. Conflicting commercial regulations of the different States shackled and diminished both foreign and domestic trade; hence the power to regulate commerce was conferred. We had a large common domain, already added by the several States for the common benefit of all; purchase and war might make large additions to this common domain; hence the power over existing and future territories, with the stipulation to admit new States, was conferred. Being independent States, in such close proximity, acts seriously affecting the tranquility of some might be done by others; fugitives from labor and justice in one might seek sanctuary in others, producing strife, and bloodshed, and insecurity; therefore the power was conferred in the common agent, and the duty imposed by the compact upon each confederate to remedy these evils. These were the main objects for forming the Federal Government; the powers it possesses were conferred chiefly with the view of securing them. How have these great duties been discharged by the Federal Government and by our confederates?

The Executive Department of the Federal Government, for forty-eight out of the first sixty years under the present Constitution, was in the hands of Southern Presidents, and so just, fair, and equitable, constitutional and advantageous to the country was the policy which they pursued, that their policy and administrations were generally maintained by the people. Certainly there was no just cause of complaint from the Northern States—no advantage was ever sought or obtained by them for their section of the Republic. They never sought to use a single one of the powers of the Government for the advancement of the local or peculiar interests of the South, and they all left office without leaving a single law on the statute-book where repeal would have affected injuriously a single industrial pursuit, or the business of a single human being in the South. But on the contrary, they had acquiesced in the adoption of a policy in the highest degree beneficial to Northern interests. The principles and policy of these Presidents were marked by the most enlarged and comprehensive statesmanship, pro-

moting the highest interests of the Republic. They enlarged
the domains of commerce by treaties with all nations, upon the
great principle of equal justice to all nations, and special favors
to none. They protected commerce and trade with an efficient
navy in every sea. Mr. Jefferson acquired Louisiana, extending
from the Balize to the British possessions on the north, and
from the Mississippi to the Pacific Ocean[2]—a country larger
than the whole United States at the time of the acknowledge-
ment of their independence. He guaranteed the protection of
the Federal Government by treaty to all the inhabitants of the
purchased territory, in their lives, liberties, property and religion—sanctioned by law the right of all the people of the
United States to emigrate into the territory with all of their
property of every kind, (expressly including slaves,) to build
up new States, and to come into the Union with such constitutions as they might choose to make. Mr. Madison vindicated
the honor of the nation, maintained the security of commerce,
and the inviolability of the persons of our sailors by the war
of 1812. Mr. Monroe acquired Florida from Spain, extending
the same guarantee to the inhabitants which Mr. Jefferson had
to those of Louisiana. General Jackson compelled France, and
other nations of Europe, to do long deferred justice to our plun-
dered merchants. Mr. Tyler acquired Texas by voluntary compact, and Mr. Polk California and New Mexico by successful
war. In all their grand additions to the wealth and power of
the Republic, these statesmen neither asked nor sought any
advantage for their own section; they admitted they were common acquisitions, purchased by the common blood and trea-

---

2. Toombs could get carried away, even about geography. The Louisiana
Purchase did indeed add a gigantic land mass, larger than the settled acreage
of the original 13 colonies, to the nation. Jefferson's purchase did indeed sweep
southwards from Canada and westwards from the Mississippi River. But the
Louisiana Purchase ended on the west at the Rockies, not at the Pacific Ocean;
and on the south at the Gulf, not at the Balize (Belize), a river/capital city in
the Central American republic of the same name.

sure, and for the common benefit of the people of the Republic, without reference to locality or institutions. Neither these statesmen nor their constituents sought in any way to use the Government for the interest of themselves or their section, or for the injury of a single member of the Confederacy. We can to-day open wide the history of their administrations and point with pride to every act, and challenge the world to point out a single act stained with injustice to the North, or with partiality to their own section. This is our record; let us now examine that of our confederates.

The instant the Government was organized, at the very first Congress, the Northern States evinced a general desire and purpose to use it for their own benefit, and to pervert its powers for sectional advantage, and they have steadily pursued that policy to this day. They demanded a monopoly of the business of ship-building, and got a prohibition against the sale of foreign ships to citizens of the United States, which exists to this day.

They demanded a monopoly of the coasting trade, in order to get higher freights than they could get in open competition with the carriers of the world. Congress gave it to them, and they yet hold this monopoly. And now, to-day, if a foreign vessel in Savannah offer[s] to take your rice, cotton, grain or lumber to New-York, or any other American port, for nothing, your laws prohibit it, in order that Northern ship-owners may get enhanced prices for doing your carrying. This same shipping interest, with cormorant rapacity, have steadily burrowed their way through your legislative halls, until they have saddled the agricultural classes with a large portion of the legitimate expenses of their own business. We pay a million of dollars per annum for the lights which guide them into and out of your ports. We built and kept up, at the cost of at least another million a year, hospitals for their sick and disabled seamen, when they wear them out and cast them ashore. We pay half a million per annum to support and bring home those they cast away in foreign lands. They demand, and have received, millions of the public money to increase the safety of harbors, and lessen the danger of navigating our rivers. All of which expenses legitimately fall upon their business, and should come out of their own pockets, instead of a common treasury.

Even the fishermen of Massachusetts and New England demand and receive from the public treasury about half a million of dollars per annum as a pure bounty on their business of catching codfish. The North, at the very first Congress, demanded and received bounties under the name of protection, for every trade, craft, and calling which they pursue, and there is not an artisan in brass, or iron, or wood, or weaver, or spinner in wool or cotton, or a calico-maker, or iron-master, or a coal-owner, in all of the Northern or Middle States, who has not received what he calls the protection of his government on his industry to the extent of from fifteen to two hundred per cent from the year 1791 to this day. They will not strike a blow, or stretch a muscle, without bounties from the government. No wonder they cry aloud for the glorious Union; they have the same reason for praising it, that craftsmen of Ephesus had for shouting, "Great is Diana of the Ephesians," whom all Asia and the world worshipped. By it they got their wealth; by it they levy tribute on honest labor. It is true that this policy has been largely sustained by the South; it is true that the present tariff was sustained by an almost unanimous vote of the South; but it was a reduction—a reduction necessary from the plethora of the revenue; but the policy of the North soon made it inadequate to meet the public expenditure, by an enormous and profligate increase of the public expenditure; and at the last session of Congress they brought in and passed through the House the most atrocious tariff bill that ever was enacted, raising the present duties from twenty to two hundred and fifty per cent above the existing rates of duty. That bill now lies on the table of the Senate. It was a master stroke of abolition policy; it united cupidity to fanaticism, and thereby made a combination which has swept the country. There were thousands of protectionists in Pennsylvania, New Jersey, New-York, and in New-England, who were not abolitionists. There were thousands of abolitionists who were free traders. The mongers brought them together upon a mutual surrender of their principles. The free-trade abolitionists became protectionists; the non-abolition protectionists became abolitionists. The result of this coalition was the infamous Morrill bill[3]—the robber and the incendiary struck hands, and united in joint raid against the South.

Thus stands the account between the North and the South. Under its ordinary and most favorable action, bounties and protection to every interest and every pursuit in the North, to the extent of at least fifty millions per annum, besides the expenditure of at least sixty millions out of every seventy of the public expenditure among them, thus making the treasury a perpetual fertilizing stream to them and their industry, and a suction-pump to drain away our substance and parch up our lands.

With these vast advantages, ordinary and extraordinary, one would have supposed the North would have been content, and would have at least respected the security and tranquility of such obedient and profitable brethren; but such is not human nature. They despised the patient victims of their avarice, and they very soon began a war upon our political rights and social institutions, marked by every act of perfidy and treachery which could add a darker hue to such a warfare. In 1820, the Northern party, (and I mean by that term now and whenever

3. A Republican-sponsored bill, named after its major congressional proponent, Justin S. Morrill of Vermont. The Morrill bill proposed somewhat higher import duties on foreign manufactured goods which would compete with American-made goods in the American market. Southerners stalled off passage of the Morrill bill in 1859–60. But in March, 1861, with seven southern states out of the Union (and thus out of Congress), northern Republicans were able to pass the Morrill bill.

else it is used, or its equivalent, in these remarks, the Anti-slavery or Abolition party of the North,) endeavored to exclude the State of Missouri from admission into the Union, because she chose to protect African slavery in the new State. In the House, where they had a majority, they rejected her application, and a struggle ensued, when some half a dozen of Northern men gave way, and admitted the State, but upon condition of the exclusion of slavery from all that country, acquired from France by the treaty of 1802, lying north of thirty-six degrees thirty minutes, north latitude, and outside of the State of Missouri.[4] This act of exclusion violated the express provisions of the treaty of 1802, to which the National faith was pledged; violated the well-settled policy of the Government, at least from Adams's administration to that day, and has, since slavery was adjudicated by the Supreme Court of the United States, violated the Constitution itself.[5] When we acquired California and New-Mexico this party, scorning all compromises and all concessions, demanded that slavery should be forever excluded from them, and all other acquisitions of the Republic, either by purchase or conquest, forever. This position of this Northern party brought about the troubles of 1850, and the political excitement of 1854. The South at all times demanded nothing but equality in the common territories, equal enjoyment of them with their property, to that extended to Northern citizens and their property—nothing more. They said, we pay our part in all the blood and treasure expended in their acquisition. Give us equality of enjoyment, equal right to expansion—it is as necessary to our prosperity as yours. In 1790 we had less than eight hundred thousand slaves. Under our mild and humane administration of the system they have increased above four millions. The country has expanded to meet this growing want, and Florida, Alabama, Mississippi, Louisiana, Texas,

4. The Louisiana Purchase Territory.
5. According to the Dred Scott decision of 1857.

Arkansas, Kentucky, Tennessee, and Missouri, have received this increasing tide of African labor; before the end of this century, at precisely the same rate of increase, the Africans among us in a subordinate condition will amount to eleven millions of persons. What shall be done with them? We must expand or perish. We are constrained by an inexorable necessity to accept expansion or extermination. Those who tell you that the territorial question is an abstraction, that you can never colonize another territory without the African slave-trade, are both deaf and blind to the history of the last sixty years. All just reasoning, all past history, condemn the fallacy. The North understand it better—they have told us for twenty years that their object was to pen up slavery within its present limits—surround it with a border of free States, and like the scorpion surrounded with fire, they will make it sting itself to death. One thing at least is certain, that whatever may be the effect of your exclusion from the Territories, there is no dispute but that the North mean it, and adopt it as a measure hostile to slavery upon this point. They all agree, they are all unanimous in Congress, in the States, on the rostrum, in the sanctuary—everywhere they declare that slavery shall not go into the Territories. They took up arms to drive it out of Kansas; and Sharpe's rifles were put into the hands of assassins by Abolition preachers to do their work. Are they mistaken? No; they are not. The party put it into their platform at Philadelphia—they have it in the corner-stone of their Chicago platform; Lincoln is on it—pledged to it.[6] Hamlin[7] is on it, and pledged to it; every Abolitionist in the Union, in or out of place, is openly pledged, in some manner, to drive us from the common Territories. This conflict, at least, is irrepressible—it is easily

6. The first two Republican National Conventions, meeting in Philadelphia in 1856 and Chicago in 1860, pledged to stop the expansion of slavery into new territories.

7. Hannibal Hamlin of Maine, Lincoln's first Vice President.

understood—we demand the equal right with the North to go into the common Territories with all of our property, slaves included, and to be there protected in its peaceable enjoyment by the Federal Government, until such Territories may come into the Union as equal States—then we admit them with or without slavery, as the people themselves may decide for themselves. Will you surrender this principle? The day you do this base, unmanly deed, you embrace political degradation and death.

But this is only one of the points of the case; the North agreed to deliver up fugitives from labor. In pursuance of this clause of the Constitution, Congress, in 1797, during Washington's administration, passed a Fugitive Slave law; that act never was faithfully respected all over the North, but it was not obstructed by State legislation until within the last thirty years; but the spirit of hostility to our rights became more active and determined, and in 1850 that act was found totally insufficient to recover and return fugitives from labor; therefore the act of 1850 was passed. The passage of that act was sufficient to rouse the demon of abolition all over the North. The pulpit, the press, abolition societies, popular assemblages, belched forth nothing but imprecations and curses upon the South and the honest men of the North who voted to maintain the Constitution. And thirteen States of the Union, by the most solemn acts of legislation, wilfully, knowingly, and corruptly perjured themselves and annulled this law within their respective limits.[8] I say wilfully, knowingly, and corruptly. The Constitution is plain—it was construed in 1793 by Washington and the Second Congress. In the Senate, the bill for the rendition of fugitives was unanimously passed, and nearly unanimously passed by the House of Representatives, and signed by Washington. All the courts of the United States, Federal

---

8. Toombs here referred to the northern Personal Liberty Laws.

and State, from the Supreme Court of the United States to the
Justice Courts of all the States whose actions have ever come
under my notice, construed this Constitution to mean and intend the rendition of fugitive slaves by law of Congress, which
might be aided, not thwarted, by State legislation, until the
decision of the Supreme Court of Wisconsin held otherwise,
and that decision was unanimously overruled by Northern and
Southern judges in the Supreme Court, and which Court, in
the same case, unanimously affirmed the constitutionality of
the act of 1850. But these acts were not only annulled by the
abolition Legislatures, but annulled under circumstances of
atrocity and aggravation unknown to the legislation of any
civilized people in the world. Some of them punish us with
penitentiary punishment as felons for even claiming our own
slaves within their limits, even by his own consent; others by
ingenious contrivances prevent the possibility of your sustaining your rights in their limits, where they seek to compel you
to go, and then punish you by fine and infamous punishments
for asserting your rights and failing to get them. This is the
fidelity of our brethren (!) to their plighted faith—their oft-
repeated oaths! Yet some excellent people among us want some
more of such securities for our rights, our peace, and security.
God Almighty have mercy on these poor people, if they listen
to such counsellors. No arm of flesh can save them. Another
one of our guarantees in the Constitution was, that fugitives
from justice, committing crimes in one State and fleeing to
another, should be delivered up by the State into which they
might flee to the authorities of the State from whence they fled
and where the crime was committed. This constitutional principle is nothing more than the law of nations necessary to the
security and tranquility of sovereignty, and so universally respected and acknowledged that we have treaties with all civilized nations by which that duty is mutually secured in all
high crimes, (political excepted,) and it is every day executed
by us and for us under their treaties. But as early as 1837 or

1838 two citizens of Maine came to Savannah, stole a slave, fled to Maine, and two successive Governors refused to deliver up the culprits, the real grievance being that they had only stolen slaves—a pious work, rather to be encouraged than punished. Georgia demanded, remonstrated, threatened, and submitted to the wrong.

It is true the Legislature authorized the Governor to call a convention of the people to take into consideration the mode of redress. But what are called moderate, wise counsels prevailed. Excellent conservative—ay, that's the word—conservative men advised us not to disturb the glorious Union about so small a matter; we submitted, and submission brought its legitimate fruits. Within a year or two after, a similar case occurred with New-York, while Seward was Governor. He refused, and attempted to cover himself under the idea that there could be no property in slaves. Virginia made the same demand on him, with like results and like submission; and from that day to this that constitutional right has been practically surrendered in the case of negro-stealing. But our Northern brethren, having in this case, as in all others, gained an inch, demanded an ell. We still fancied that if this provision of the Constitution would no longer protect our property, it would protect our lives. Vain and foolish hope! Last year John Brown made a raid on Virginia. He went with torch and rifle, with the purpose of subverting her government, exciting insurrection among her slaves, and murdering her peaceable inhabitants; he succeeded only in committing murder and arson and treason. One of his accomplices (a son) escaped to Ohio, was demanded, and the Governor of Ohio refused to give him up; another fled to Iowa; he, too, was demanded, and refused. It is true both of these miscreants (the Governors of these States) attempted to cover their plain violation of the Constitution and their oaths with flimsy pretexts about formalities, but they failed to hide from us the great fact that it was sympathy with the cause of John Brown which gave sanctuary to his confed-

erates. If these men had have fled to Great Britain or France,
we would have received them back and inflicted upon them the
just punishment for their infamous crimes under our treaties.
But they were wiser; they fled among our brethren; we had no
treaty with them; we had only a Constitution and their oaths
of fidelity to it. It failed us, and their murderers are free, ready
again to apply the incendiary's torch to your dwelling and the
assassin's knife and the poisoned bowl to you and your family.
Do you not love these brethren? Oh! what a glorious Union!
especially "to insure domestic tranquility."

I have shown you what this party has done, and declared
in the national councils, in the State Legislatures, by and
through their executive departments. Let us examine what
they are at as private citizens. By the laws of nations, founded
on natural justice, no nation, nor the subjects or citizens of any
nation, have the right to disturb the peace or security of any
other nation or people, much less to conspire, excite insurrection, discontent, or the commission of crimes among them, and
all these are held to be good causes of war. For twenty years
this party has, by Abolition societies, by publications made by
them, by the public press, through the pulpit and their own
legislative halls, and every effort—by reproaches, by abuse, by
vilification, by slander—to disturb our security, our tranquillity—to excite discontent between the different classes of our
people, and to excite our slaves to insurrection. No nation in
the world would submit to such conduct from any other nation.
I will not willingly do so from this Abolition party. I demand
the protection of my State government, to whom I own my
allegiance. I wish it distinctly understood that it is the price
of my allegiance. You are here, constitutional legislators—I
make the demand to-day of you. Gentlemen, I have thus shown
you the violations of our constitutional rights by our confederates; I have shown you that they are plain, palpable, deliberate, and dangerous; that they are committed by the executive,
legislative, and judicial departments of the State governments

of our confederates—that all their wrongs are approved by the people of these States. I say the time has come to redress these acknowledged wrongs, and to avert even greater evils, of which these are but the signs and symbols. But I am asked, why do you demand action now? The question is both appropriate and important; it ought to be frankly met. The Abolitionists say you are raising a clamor because you were beaten in the election. The falsity of this statement needs no confirmation. Look to our past history for its refutation. Some excellent citizens and able men in Georgia say the election of any man constitutionally is no cause for a dissolution of the Union. That position is calculated only to mislead, and not to enlighten. It is not the issue. I say the election of Lincoln, with all of its surroundings, is sufficient. What is the significance of his election? It is the indorsement, by the non-slaveholding States, of all those acts of aggression upon our rights by all these States, legislatures, governors, judges, and people. He is elected by the perpetrators of these wrongs with the purpose and intent to aid and support them in wrong-doing.

Hitherto the Constitution has had on its side the Federal Executive, whose duty it is to execute the laws and Constitution against these malefactors. It has earnestly endeavored to discharge that duty. Relying upon its power and good faith to remedy these wrongs, we have listened to conservative counsels, trusting to time, to the Federal Executive, and to a returning sense of justice in the North. The Executive has been faithful—the Federal judiciary have been faithful—the President has appointed sound judges, sound marshals, and other subordinate officers to interpret and to execute the laws. With the best intentions, they have all failed—our property has been stolen, our people murdered; felons and assassins have found sanctuary in the arms of the party which elected Mr. Lincoln. The Executive power, the last bulwark of the Constitution to defend us against these enemies of the Constitution, has been swept away, and we now stand without a shield, with bare bosoms presented to our enemies, and we demand at your hands the sword for our defence, and if you will not give it to us, we will take it—take it by the divine right of self-defence, which governments neither give nor can take away. Therefore, redress for past and present wrongs demands resistance to the rule of Lincoln and his Abolition horde over us; he comes at their head to shield and protect them in the perpetration of these outrages upon us, and, what is more, he comes at their head to aid them in consummating their avowed purposes by the power of the Federal Government. Their main purpose, as indicated by all their acts of hostility to slavery, is its final and total abolition. His party declare it; their acts prove it. He has declared it; I accept his declaration. The battle of the irrepressible conflict has hitherto been fought on his side alone. We demand service in this war. Surely no one will deny that the election of Lincoln is the indorsement of the policy of those who elected him, and an indorsement of his own opinions. The opinions of those who elected him are to be found in their solemn acts under oath—in their State governments, indorsed by their constituents. To them I have already referred. They are also to be found in the votes of his supporters in Congress—also indorsed by the party, by their return. Their opinions are to be found in the speeches of Seward, and Sumner, and Lovejoy, and their associates and confederates in the two Houses of Congress.[9] Since the promotion of Mr. Lincoln's party, all of them speak with one voice, and speak trumpet-tongued their fixed purpose to outlaw four thousand millions of our property in the Territories, and to put it under the ban of the empire in the States where it exists. They declare their purpose to war against slavery until there shall not be a slave in America, and until the African is elevated to a social and political

9. Republicans William H. Seward of New York, Charles Sumner of Massachusetts, and Owen Lovejoy of Illinois, whose brother Elijah P. Lovejoy was killed by an anti-abolitionist mob.

equality with the white man. Lincoln indorses them and their principles, and in his own speeches declares the conflict irrepressible and enduring, until slavery is everywhere abolished.

Hitherto they have carried on this warfare by State action, by individual action, by appropriation, by the incendiary's torch and the poisoned bowl. They were compelled to adopt this method because the Federal executive and the Federal judiciary were against them. They will have possession of the Federal executive with its vast power, patronage, prestige of legality, its army, its navy, and its revenue on the fourth of March next. Hitherto it has been on the side of the Constitution and the right; after the fourth of March it will be in the hands of your enemy. Will you let him have it? (Cries of "No, no. Never.") Then strike while it is yet today. Withdraw your sons from the army, from the navy, and every department of the Federal public service. Keep your own taxes in your own coffers—buy arms with them and throw the bloody spear into this den of incendiaries and assassins, and let God defend the right. But you are advised to wait, send soft messages to their brethren, to beg them to relent, to give you some assurances of their better fidelity for the future. What more can you get from them under this Government? You have the Constitution—you have its exposition by themselves for seventy years—you have their oaths—they have broken all these, and will break them again. They tell you everywhere, loudly and defiantly, you shall have no power, no security until you give up the right of governing yourselves according to your own will—until you submit to theirs. For this is the meaning of Mr. Lincoln's irrepressible conflict—this is his emphatic declaration to all the world. Will you heed it? For myself, like the Athenian ambassador, I will take no security but this, that it shall not be in the power of our enemies to injure my country if they desire it. Nothing but ruin will follow delay. The enemy on the fourth of March will intrench himself behind a quintuple wall of defence. Executive power, judiciary, (Mr. Seward has already proclaimed its reformation,) army, navy, and treasury. Twenty years of labor, and toil, and taxes all expended upon preparation, would not make up for the advantage your enemies would gain if the rising sun on the fifth of March should find you in the Union. Then strike while it is yet time.

But we are told that secession would destroy the fairest fabric of liberty the world ever saw, and that we are the most prosperous people in the world under it. The arguments of tyranny as well as its acts, always reenact themselves. The arguments I now hear in favor of this Northern connection are identical in substance, and almost in the same words as those which were used in 1775 and 1776 to sustain the British connection. We won liberty, sovereignty, and independence by the American Revolution—we endeavored to secure and perpetuate these blessings by means of our Constitution. The very men who use these arguments admit that this Constitution, this compact, is violated, broken and trampled under foot by the abolition party. Shall we surrender the jewels because their robbers and incendiaries have broken the casket? Is this the way to preserve liberty? I would as lief surrender it back to the British crown as to the abolitionists. I will defend it from both. Our purpose is to defend those liberties. What baser fate could befall us or this great experiment of free government than to have written upon its tomb: "Fell by the hands of abolitionists and the cowardice of its natural defenders." If we quail now, this will be its epitaph.

We are said to be a happy and prosperous people. We have been, because we have hitherto maintained our ancient rights and liberties—we will be until we surrender them. They are in danger; come, freemen, to the rescue. If we are prosperous, it is due to God, ourselves, and the wisdom of our State government. We have an executive, legislative, and judicial department at home, possessing and entitled to the confidence of the people. I have already vainly asked for the law of the Federal Government that promotes our prosperity. I have shown you many that retard that prosperity—many that drain our coffers for the benefit of our bitterest foes. I say bitterest foes— show me the nation in the world that hates, despises, villifies, or plunders us like our abolition "brethren" in the North. There is none. I can go to England or France, or any other country in Europe with my slave, without molestation or violating any law. I can go anywhere except in my own country, whilom[10] called "the glorious Union;" here alone am I stigmatized as a felon; here alone am I an outlaw; here alone am I under the ban of the empire; here alone I have neither security nor tranquillity; here alone are organized governments ready to protect the incendiary, the assassin who burns my dwelling or takes my life or those of my wife and children; here alone are hired emissaries paid by brethren to glide through the domestic circle and intrigue insurrection with all of its nameless horrors. My countrymen, "if you have nature in you, bear it not." Withdraw yourselves from such a confederacy; it is your right to do so— your duty to do so. I know not why the abolitionists should object to it, unless they want to torture and plunder you. If they resist this great sovereign right, make another war of independence, for that then will be the question; fight its battles over again—reconquer liberty and independence. As for me, I will take any place in the great conflict for rights which you may assign. I will take none in the Federal Government during Mr. Lincoln's administration.

If you desire a Senator after the fourth of March, you must elect one in my place. I have served you in the State and national councils for nearly a quarter of a century without once losing your confidence. I am yet ready for the public service, when honor and duty call. I will serve you anywhere where it will not degrade and dishonor my country. Make my name infamous forever, if you will, but save Georgia. I have pointed

10. Archaic word, meaning "at one time."

out your wrongs, your danger, your duty. You have claimed
nothing but that rights be respected and that justice be done.
Emblazon it on your banner—fight for it, win it, or perish in
the effort.

3

Alexander H. Stephens's Unionist Speech, Wednesday Evening, November 14

If Robert Toombs had Thomas R. R. Cobb's impulsiveness without Cobb's controls, Alexander Stephens had Cobb's controls without the impulsiveness. No two upper class Georgians differed more than the unsteady Toombs and the sustained Stephens. Toombs was hefty, over 200 pounds. Stephens was misshapen, under 95 pounds. While Toombs's figure and voice exuded masculine charisma, Stephens had the hairless face of a boy and the higher-pitched tones of a woman.

So, too, where Toombs had been born to wealth and ease, Stephens had been an impoverished orphan. While Toombs had been a brawling troublemaker at the University of Georgia, once suspended and finally expelled, Stephens had marched relentlessly to a distinguished graduation. Where Toombs was a popular "good old southern boy," Stephens was a lonely, abstracted warrior.

Yet these opposite personalities shared an intimate friendship. They fought many political battles together: as Whigs, baiting the Democrats in the 1840s; as Unionists, joining Howell

*Cobb in routing the Georgia States' Righters after the Compro-
mise of 1850; as converted Democrats, denouncing the Yankees
in the mid-1850s. No matter that Toombs became much wealth-
ier, nor that he was promoted to the Senate while Stephens
remained in the House. The two lived close to each other, enjoyed
each other's company as opposites often do, and shared fury at
those who challenged their latest mutual position.*

*Stephens retired from politics in 1859. He returned in 1860,
for the first time on a different side from Toombs's. When he
rose to speak on November 14, 1860, Stephens had everything
going for him: in Unionism, the perfect cause for his lifelong
conservatism; in his knowledge of Toombs, the perfect under-
standing of how to bait the emotional revolutionary; in the Milledgeville occasion, the perfect stage to surpass Toombs as the
star Georgian. Toombs, good fellow to the last, could only offer
three cheers, after his old friend and new antagonist scored a
stunning oratorical triumph.*[1]

FELLOW-CITIZENS: I appear before you to-night at the
request of members of the Legislature and others, to speak of
matters of the deepest interest that can possibly concern us all,
of an earthly character. There is nothing,—no question or subject connected with this life, that concerns a free people so
intimately as that of the Government under which they live.
We are now, indeed, surrounded by evils. Never, since I entered
upon the public stage, has the country been so environed with
difficulties and dangers that threatened the public peace and
the very existence of society as now. I do not appear before you

---

1. The latest biography is Thomas E. Schott, *Alexander H. Stephens of
Georgia: A Biography* (Baton Rouge, 1988). We have transcribed Stephens's
speech from Richard M. Johnston and William H. Browne, *Life of Alexander
H. Stephens* (Philadelphia, 1878), pp. 564–80.

at my own instance. It is not to gratify any desire of my own that I am here. Had I consulted my own ease and pleasure, I should not be before you; but believing that it is the duty of every good citizen, when called on, to give his counsels and views whenever the country is in danger, as the best policy to be pursued, I am here. For these reasons, and these only, do I bespeak a calm, patient, and attentive hearing.

My object is not to stir up strife, but to allay it; not to appeal to your passions, but to your reason. Good governments can never be built up or sustained by the impulse of passion. I wish to address myself to your good sense, to your good judgement, and if, after hearing, you disagree, let us agree to disagree, and part as we met, friends. We all have the same object, the same interest. That people should disagree in republican governments upon questions of public policy is natural. That men should disagree upon all matters connected with human investigation, whether relating to science or human conduct, is natural. Hence in free governments parties will arise. But a free people should express their different opinions with liberality and charity, with no acrimony toward those of their fellows when honestly and sincerely given. These are my feelings to-night.

Let us, therefore, reason together. It is not my purpose to say aught to wound the feelings of any individual who may be present; and if, in the ardency with which I shall express my opinions, I shall say anything which may be deemed too strong, let it be set down to the zeal with which I advocate my own convictions. There is with me no intention to irritate or offend.

Fellow-citizens, we are all launched in the same bark; we are all in the same craft in the wide political ocean,—the same destiny awaits us all for weal or woe. We have been launched in the good old ship that has been upon the waves for three-quarters of a century, which has been in so many tempests and storms, has been many times in peril, and patriots have often feared that they should have to give it up:

ay, have at times almost given it up; but still the gallant
ship is afloat. Though new storms now howl around us, and
the tempest beats heavily against us, I say to you, Don't give
up the ship,—don't abandon her yet. If she can possibly be
preserved, and our rights, interests, and security be maintained, the object is worth the effort. Let us not, on account
of disappointment and chagrin at the reverse of an election,
give up all as lost; but let us see what can be done to prevent
a wreck. (*A voice.*—"The ship has holes in her.") And there
may be leaks in her, but let us stop them if we can; many
a stout old ship has been saved with richest cargo after many
leaks; and it may be so now.

I do not intend, on this occasion, to enter into the history
of the reasons or causes of the embarrassments which press so
heavily upon us all at this time. In justice to myself, however,
I must barely state upon this point that I do think much of it
depended upon ourselves. The consternation that has come
upon the people is the result of a sectional election of a President of the United States, one whose opinions and avowed
principles are in antagonism to our interests and rights, and
we believe, if carried out, would subvert the Constitution under
which we now live. But are we entirely blameless in this matter, my countrymen? I give it to you as my opinion, that but
for the policy the Southern people pursued, this fearful result
would not have occurred. Mr. Lincoln has been elected, I doubt
not, by a minority of the people of the United States. What will
be the extent of that minority we do not yet know, but the
disclosure, when made, will show, I think, that a majority of
the constitutional conservative voters of the country were
against him; and had the South stood firmly in the Convention
at Charleston, on her old platform of principles of nonintervention, there is in my mind but little doubt that whoever
might have been the candidate of the national Democratic
party would have been elected by as large a majority as that

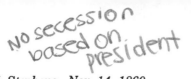

No secession based on president

which elected Mr. Buchanan or Mr. Pierce.[2] Therefore let us not be hasty and rash in our action, especially if the result be attributable at all to ourselves. Before looking to extreme measures, let us see, as Georgians, that everything which can be done to preserve our rights, our interests, and our honor, as well as the peace of the country in the Union, be first done.

The first question that presents itself is, Shall the people of the South secede from the Union in consequence of the election of Mr. Lincoln to the Presidency of the United States? My countrymen, I tell you frankly, candidly, and earnestly, that I do not think they ought. In my judgment, the election of no man, constitutionally chosen to that high office, is sufficient cause for any State to separate from the Union. It ought to stand by and aid still in maintaining the Constitution of the country. To make a point of resistance to the Government, to withdraw from it because a man has been constitutionally elected, puts us in the wrong. We are pledged to maintain the Constitution. Many of us have sworn to support it. Can we, therefore, for the mere election of a man to the Presidency, and that too in accordance with the prescribed forms of the Constitution, make a point of resistance to the Government, without becoming the breakers of that sacred instrument ourselves by withdrawing ourselves from it? Would we not be in the wrong? Whatever fate is to befall this country, let it never be laid to the charge of the people of the South, and especially to the people of Georgia, that we were untrue to our national

2. At the Democratic National Convention in Charleston in 1860, the Lower South demanded a platform plank endorsing congressional *intervention*, to protect slavery in national territories. Previous Democratic Conventions, which had nominated Franklin Pierce in 1852 and James Buchanan in 1856, had instead endorsed the principle of congressional *nonintervention*. Those previous platforms had left the decision on slavery to settlers in the territories. The Lower South's provocative new insistence on congressional *intervention* to protect slavery led to the split of the Democratic Party in Charleston.

engagements. Let the fault and the wrong rest upon others. If all our hopes are to be blasted, if the Republic is to go down, let us be found to the last moment standing on the deck with the Constitution of the United States waving over our heads. Let the fanatics of the North break the Constitution, if such is their fell purpose. Let the responsibility be upon them. I shall presently speak more of their acts; but let not the South—let us not be the ones to commit the aggression. We went into the election with this people. The result was different from what we wished; but the election has been constitutionally held. Were we to make a point of resistance to the Government and go out of the Union on that account, the record would be made up hereafter against us.

But it is said that Mr. Lincoln's policy and principles are against the Constitution, and that, if he carries them out, it will be destructive of our rights. Let us not anticipate a threatened evil. If he violates the Constitution, then will come our time to act. Do not let *us* break it, because, forsooth, *he* may. If he does, that is the time for us to strike. I think it would be injudicious and unwise to do this sooner. I do not anticipate that Mr. Lincoln will do anything to jeopard[ize] our safety or security, whatever may be his spirit to do it; for he is bound by the constitutional checks which are thrown around him, which at this time render him powerless to do any great mischief. This shows the wisdom of our system. The President of the United States is no emperor, no dictator,—he is clothed with no absolute power. He can do nothing unless he is backed by power in Congress. The House of Representatives is largely in a majority against him. In the very face and teeth of the heavy majority which he has obtained in the Northern States, there have been large gains in the House of Representatives to the Conservative Constitutional party of the country, which here I will call the National Democratic party, because that is the cognomen it has at the North. There are twelve of this party elected from New York to the next Congress, I believe.

In the present House there are but four, I think. In Pennsylvania, New Jersey, Ohio, and Indiana there have been gains. In the present Congress there were one hundred and thirteen Republicans, when it takes one hundred and seventeen to make a majority. The gains in the Democratic party in Pennsylvania, Ohio, New Jersey, New York, Indiana, and other States, notwithstanding its distractions, have been enough to make a majority of near thirty in the next House against Mr. Lincoln. Even in Boston, Mr. Burlingame, one of the noted leaders of the fanatics of that section, has been defeated and a conservative man returned in his stead.[3] Is this the time, then, to apprehend that Mr. Lincoln, with this large majority in the House of Representatives against him, can carry out any of his unconstitutional principles in that body?

In the Senate he will also be powerless. There will be a majority of four against him. This, after the loss of Bigler, Fitch, and others, by the unfortunate dissensions of the National Democratic party in their States.[4] Mr. Lincoln cannot appoint an officer without the consent of the Senate,—he cannot form a cabinet without the same consent. He will be in the condition of George the Third (the embodiment of Toryism), who had to ask the Whigs to appoint his ministers, and was compelled to receive a cabinet utterly opposed to his views;[5] and so Mr. Lincoln will be compelled to ask of the Senate to choose for him a cabinet, if the Democracy of that party chose to put him on such terms. He will be compelled to do this or let the Gov-

3. Anson Burlingame was a three-term Republican congressman from Massachusetts who was unseated by the Democrats' William Appleton in 1860. Burlingame was especially notorious for almost fighting a duel with Preston Brooks of South Carolina, after Brooks's brutal caning of Senator Charles Sumner of Massachusetts in 1856.
4. United States Senators William Bigler of Pennsylvania and Graham Fitch of New York, both Democrats, both lately denied reelection, in part because of Democratic factional divisions in their respective states.
5. The king of England in the period before the American Revolution.

ernment stop, if the National Democratic men—the conservative men in the Senate—should so determine. Then how can Mr. Lincoln obtain a cabinet which would aid him, or allow him, to violate the Constitution[?] Why, then, I say, should we disrupt the ties of the Union when his hands are tied,—when he can do nothing against us?

I have heard it mooted that no man in the State of Georgia who is true to her interests could hold office under Mr. Lincoln. But I ask who appoints to office? Not the President alone; the Senate has to concur. No man can be appointed without the consent of the Senate. Should any man, then, refuse to hold office that was given him by a Democratic Senate?

(Mr. Toombs interrupted, and said, if the Senate was Democratic, it was for Breckenridge.)

Well, then (continued Mr. Stephens), I apprehend that no man could be justly considered untrue to the interests of Georgia, or incur any disgrace, if the interests of Georgia required it, to hold an office which a Breckenridge Senate had given him, even though Mr. Lincoln should be President. (Applause.)

I trust, my countrymen, you will be still and silent. I am addressing your good sense. I am giving you my views in a calm and dispassionate manner, and if any of you differ from me, you can on some other occasion give your views, as I am doing now, and let reason and true patriotism decide between us. In my judgment, I say, under such circumstances, there would be no possible disgrace for a Southern man to hold office. No man will be suffered to be appointed, I have no doubt, who is not true to the Constitution, if Southern Senators are true to their trusts, as I cannot permit myself to doubt that they will be.

My honorable friend who addressed you last night (Mr. Toombs), and to whom I listened with the profoundest attention, asks if we would submit to Black Republican rule? I say to you and to him, as a Georgian, I never would submit to any Black Republican aggression upon our Constitutional rights.

I will never myself consent, as much as I admire this Union, for the glories of the past or the blessings of the present, as much as it has done for civilisation[sic]; as much as the hopes of the world hang upon it; I would never submit to aggression upon my rights to maintain it longer; and if they cannot be maintained in the Union standing on the Georgia platform, where I have stood from the time of its adoption, I would be in favor of disrupting every tie which binds the States together. I will have equality for Georgia and for the citizens of Georgia in this Union, or I will look for new safeguards elsewhere. This is my position. The only question now is, Can this be secured in the Union? This is what I am counselling with you to-night about. Can it be secured? In my judgment it may be; but it may not be; but let us do all we can, so that in the future, if the worst comes, it may never be said we were negligent in doing our duty to the last.

My countrymen, I am not of those who believe the Union has been a curse up to this time. True men, men of integrity, entertain different views from me on this subject. I do not question their right to do so: I would not impugn their motives in so doing. Nor will I undertake to say that this Government of our fathers is perfect. There is nothing perfect in this world of human origin; nothing connected with human nature from man himself to any of his works. You may select the wisest and best men for your judges, and yet how many defects are there in the administration of justice! You may select the wisest and best men for your legislators, and yet how many defects are apparent in your laws! And it is so in our Government. But that this Government of our fathers, with all its defects, comes nearer the objects of all good governments than any other on the face of the earth, is my settled conviction. Contrast it now with any other.

("England," said Mr. Toombs.)

England, my friend says. Well, that is the next best, I grant; but I think we have improved upon England. Statesmen

tried their 'prentice hand on the Government of England, and
then ours was made. Ours sprung from that, avoiding many of
its defects, taking most of the good, and leaving out many of
its errors; and from the whole our fathers constructed and built
up this model republic,—the best which the history of the world
gives any account of. Compare, my friends, this Government
with that of France, Spain, Mexico, the South American republics, Germany, Ireland, Prussia; or, if you travel farther
east, to Turkey or China. Where will you go, following the sun
in his circuit round our globe, to find a government that better
protects the liberties of its people and secures to them the
blessings we enjoy? I think that one of the evils that beset us
is a surfeit of liberty, an exuberance of the priceless blessings
for which we are ungrateful. We listened to my honorable friend
who addressed you last night (Mr. Toombs) as he recounted the
evils of this Government. The first was the fishing-bounties,
paid mostly to the sailors of New England. Our friend stated
that forty-eight years of our Government were under the
administration of Southern Presidents. Well, these fishing-
bounties began under the rule of a Southern President, I believe. No one of them, during the whole forty-eight years, ever
set his Administration against the principle or policy of them.
It is not for me to say whether it was a wise policy in the
beginning; it probably was not, and I have not a word to say
in its defence. But the reason given for it was to encourage our
young men to go to sea and learn to manage ships. We had at
that time but a small navy. It was thought best to encourage
a class of our people to become acquainted with seafaring life;
to become sailors, to man our navy. It requires practice to walk
the deck of a ship, to pull the ropes, to furl the sails, to go aloft,
to climb the mast; and it was thought that by offering this
bounty a nursery might be formed in which young men would
become perfected in these arts, and it applied to one section of
the country as well as another. The result of this was, that in
the war of 1812 our sailors, many of whom came from this

nursery, were equal to any that England brought against us. At any rate, no small part of the glories of that war were gained by the veteran tars of America, and the object of these bounties was to foster that branch of the national defence. My opinion is, that whatever may have been the reason at first, this bounty ought to be discontinued,—the reason for it at first no longer exists. A bill for this object did pass the Senate the last congress I was in, to which my honorable friend contributed greatly, but it was not reached in the House of Representatives. I trust that he will yet see that he may with honor continue his connection with the Government, and that his eloquence, unrivalled in the Senate, may hereafter, as heretofore, be displayed in having this bounty, so obnoxious to him, wiped off from the statute-book.

The next evil that my friend complained of was the tariff. Well, let us look at that for a moment. About the time I commenced noticing public matters this question was agitating the country almost as fearfully as the Slave question now is. In 1832, when I was in college, South Carolina was ready to nullify or secede from the Union on this account.[6] And what have we seen? The tariff no longer distracts the public councils. Reason has triumphed. The present tariff was voted for by Massachusetts and South Carolina.[7] The lion and the lamb lay down together,—every man in the Senate and House from Massachusetts and South Carolina, I think, voted for it, as did my honorable friend himself. And if it be true, to use the figure of speech of my honorable friend, that every man in the North that works in iron and brass and wood has his muscle strength-

6. The South Carolina Nullification Controversy of 1832, in which South Carolina threatened to stop a high protective tariff from being enforced in the state, and President Andrew Jackson threatened to hang the nullifier who blocked tariff enforcement. The crisis was resolved peacefully with the Compromise Tariff of 1833, which called for lower tariffs.

7. Stephens here referred to another compromise tariff, the Tariff of 1857.

ened by the protection of the Government, that stimulant was given by his vote, and I believe that of every other Southern man. So we ought not to complain of that.

(**MR. TOOMBS**—"That tariff lessened the duties.")

Yes, and Massachusetts, with unanimity, voted with the South to lessen them, and they were made just as low as Southern men asked them to be, and those are the rates they are now at. If reason and argument with experience produced such changes in the sentiments of Massachusetts from 1832 to 1857 on the subject of the tariff, may not like changes be effected there by the same means, reason and argument, and appeals to patriotism on the present vexed question? And who can say that by 1875 or 1890 Massachusetts may not vote with South Carolina and Georgia upon all those questions that now distract the country and threaten its peace and existence? I believe in the power and efficiency of truth, in the omnipotence of truth, and its ultimate triumph when properly wielded.

Another matter of grievance alluded to by my honorable friend was the navigation laws. This policy was also commenced under the Administration of one of those Southern Presidents who ruled so well, and has been continued through all of them since. The gentleman's views of the policy of these laws and my own do not disagree. We occupied the same ground in relation to them in Congress. It is not my purpose to defend them now. But it is proper to state some matters connected with their origin.

One of the objects was to build up a commercial American marine by giving American bottoms the exclusive carrying trade between our own ports. This is a great arm of national power. The object was accomplished. We have now an amount of shipping not only coastwise but to foreign countries which puts us in the front ranks of the nations of the world. England can no longer be styled the mistress of the seas. What American is not proud of the result? Whether those laws should be continued is another question. But one thing is certain, no President, Northern or Southern, has ever yet recommended their repeal. And my friend's effort to get them repealed has met with but little favor North or South.

These, then, were the three grievances or grounds of complaint against the general system of our Government and its workings: I mean the administration of the Federal Government. As to the acts of several of the States I shall speak presently, but these three were the main ones urged against the common head. Now suppose it be admitted that all of these are evils in the system, do they overbalance and outweigh the advantages and great good which this same Government affords in a thousand innumberable ways that cannot be estimated? Have we not at the South, as well as at the North, grown great, prosperous, and happy under its operation? Has any part of the world ever shown such rapid progress in the development of wealth and all the material resources of national power and greatness as the Southern States have under the General Government, notwithstanding all its defects?

(**MR. TOOMBS.**—"In spite of it.")

My honorable friend says we have, in spite of the General Government: that without it I suppose he thinks we might have done as well or perhaps better than we have done. This grand result is in spite of the Government? That may be, and it may not be; but the great fact that we have grown great and powerful under the Government as it exists is admitted. There is no conjecture or speculation about that; it stands out bold, high, and prominent like your Stone Mountain,[8] to which the gentleman alluded in illustrating home-facts in his record,—this great fact of our unrivalled prosperity in the Union as it is admitted,—whether all this is in spite of the Government,— whether we of the South would have been better off without

8. The prominent Georgia mountain near Atlanta, destined to be, in the late twentieth century, the site of a brilliant Confederate Memorial, the southern equivalent of Mount Rushmore.

the Government, is, to say the least, problematical. On the one side we can only put the fact against speculation and conjecture on the other. But even as a question of speculation I differ from my distinguished friend. What we would have lost in border wars without the Union, or what we have gained simply by the peace it has secured, is not within our power to estimate. Our foreign trade, which is the foundation of all our prosperity, has the protection of the navy which drove the pirates from the waters near our coast where they had been buccaneering for centuries before, and might have been still, had it not been for the American navy under the command of such a spirit as Commodore Porter.[9] Now that the coast is clear, that our commerce flows freely, outwardly and inwardly, we cannot well estimate how it would have been under other circumstances. The influence of the Government on us is like that of the atmosphere around us. Its benefits are so silent and unseen that they are seldom thought of or appreciated.

We seldom think of the single element of oxygen in the air we breathe, and yet let this simple unseen and unfelt agent be withdrawn, this life-giving element be taken away from this all-pervading fluid around us, and what instant and appalling changes would take place in all organic creation!

It may be that we are all that we are "in spite of the General Government," but it may be that without it we should have been far different from what we are now. It is true there is no equal part of the earth with natural resources superior to ours. That portion of the country known as the Southern States, stretching from the Chesapeake to the Rio Grande, is fully equal to the picture drawn by the honorable and eloquent Senator last night in all natural capacities. But how many ages, centuries, passed before these capacities were developed to reach this advanced stage of civilization? There these same

9. David D. Porter, a lieutenant in the American navy and a world-wide commodore of international trading vessels.

hills rich in ore, these same rivers, valleys, and plains, are as they have been since they came from the hand of the Creator. Uneducated and uncivilized man roamed over them, for how long no history informs us.

It was only under our institutions that they could be developed. Their development is the result of the enterprise of our people under operations of the Government and institutions under which we have lived. Even our people, without these, never would have done it. The organization of society has much to do with the development of the natural resources of any country or any land. The institutions of a people, political and moral, are the matrix in which the germ of their organic structure quickens into life, takes root, and develops in form, nature, and character. Our institutions constitute the basis, the matrix, from which spring all our characteristics of development and greatness. Look at Greece! There is the same fertile soil, the same blue sky, the same inlets and harbors, the same AEgean, the same Olympus,—there is the same land where Homer sang, where Pericles spoke,—it is in nature the same old Greece; but it is living Greece no more!

Descendants of the same people inhabit the country; yet what is the reason of this mighty difference? In the midst of present degradation we see the glorious fragments of ancient works of art,—temples with ornaments and inscriptions that excite wonder and admiration, the remains of a once high order of civilization, which have outlived the language they spoke. Upon them all *Ichabod* is written,—their glory has departed.[10] Why is this so? I answer, their institutions have been destroyed. These were but the fruits of their forms of government, the matrix from which their grand development sprang; and when

---

10. Stephens probably here referred to John Greenleaf Whittier's poem "Ichabod," published in 1850. Ichabod meant "inglorious" in Hebrew; and Whittier, a Massachusetts antislavery figure, used the verse to deplore Daniel Webster's "sad concessions" to the slaveholders during the Compromise of 1850.

once the institutions of our people shall have been destroyed, there is no earthly power that can bring back the Promethean spark to kindle them here again, any more than in that ancient land of eloquence, poetry, and song. The same may be said of Italy. Where is Rome, once the mistress of the world? There are the same seven hills now, the same soil, the same natural resources; nature is the same; but what a ruin of human greatness meets the eye of the traveller throughout the length and breadth of that most down-trodden land! Why have not the people of that Heaven-favored clime the spirit that animated their fathers? Why this sad difference? It is the destruction of her institutions that has caused it. And, my countrymen, if we shall in an evil hour rashly pull down and destroy those institutions, which the patriotic hand of our fathers labored so long and so hard to build up, and which have done so much for us and for the world, who can venture the prediction that similar results will not ensue? Let us avoid them if we can. I trust the spirit is among us that will enable us to do it. Let us not rashly try the experiment of change, of pulling down and destroying, for, as in Greece and Italy, and the South American republics, and in every other place, whenever our liberty is once lost, it may never be restored to us again.

There are defects in our Government, errors in our adminstration, and shortcomings of many kinds, but in spite of these defects and errors Georgia has grown to be a great State. Let us pause here for a moment. In 1850 there was a great crisis, but not so fearful as this, for of all I have ever passed through this is the most perilous, and requires to be met with the greatest calmness and deliberation.

There were many among us in 1850 zealous to go at once out of the Union,—to disrupt every tie that binds us together. Now do you believe, had that policy been carried out at that time, we would have been the same great people that we are to-day? It may be that we would, but have you any assurance of that fact? Would we have made the same advancement, improvement, and progress in all that constitutes material wealth and prosperity that we have?

I notice in the Comptroller-General's report that the taxable property of Georgia is six hundred and seventy million dollars and upwards,—an amount not far from double what it was in 1850. I think I may venture to say that for the last ten years the material wealth of the people of Georgia has been nearly, if not quite, doubled. The same may be said of our advance in education and everything that marks our civilization. Have we any assurance that had we regarded the earnest but misguided patriotic advice, as I think, of some of that day, and disrupted the ties which bind us to the Union, we would have advanced as we have? I think not. Well, then, let us be careful now before we attempt any rash experiment of this sort. I know that there are friends whose patriotism I do not intend to question who think this Union a curse, and that we should be better off without it. I do not so think; if we can bring about a correction of those evils which threaten,—and I am not without hope that this may yet be done,—this appeal to go out with all the promises for good that accompany it, I look upon as great, and, I fear, a fatal temptation.

When I look around and see our prosperity in everything,— agriculture, commerce, art, science, and every department of progress, physical, moral, and mental,—certainly, in the face of such an exhibition, if we can, without the loss of power, or any essential right or interest, remain in the Union, it is our duty to ourselves and to posterity to do so. Let us not unwisely yield to this temptation. Our first parents, the great progenitors of the human race, were not without a like temptation when in the garden of Eden. They were led to believe that their condition would be bettered, that their eyes would be opened, and that they would become as gods. They in an evil hour yielded,—instead of becoming gods they only saw their own nakedness.

I look upon this country with our institutions as the Eden

of the world, the Paradise of the universe. It may be that out of it we may become greater and more prosperous; but I am candid and sincere in telling you that I fear if we yield to passion, and without sufficient cause shall take that step, instead of becoming greater, more peaceful, prosperous, and happy,—instead of becoming gods, we shall become demons, and at no distant day commence cutting one another's throats. This is my apprehension. Let us, therefore, whatever we do, meet these difficulties, great as they are, like wise and sensible men, and consider them in the light of all the consequences which may attend our action. Let us see first, clearly, where the path of duty leads, and then we may not fear to tread therein.

I come now to the main question put to me, and on which my counsel has been asked. That is, what the present Legislature should do in view of the dangers that threaten us, and the wrongs that have been done us by several of our confederate States in the Union, by the acts of their Legislatures nullifying the Fugitive Slave Law, and in direct disregard of their constitutional obligations? What I shall say will not be in the spirit of dictation. It will simply be my own judgment for what it is worth. It proceeds from a strong conviction that, according to it, our rights, interest, and honor,—our present safety and future security can be maintained without yet looking to the last resort, the "*ultima ratio regum.*" That should not be looked to until all else fails. That may come. On this point I am hopeful, but not sanguine. But let us use every patriotic effort to prevent it while there is ground for hope.

If any view that I may present, in your judgment, be inconsistent with the best interest of Georgia, I ask you as patriots not to regard it. After hearing me and others whom you have advised with, act in the premises according to your own convictions of duty as patriots. I speak now particularly to the members of the Legislature present. There are, as I have said, great dangers ahead. Great dangers may come from the election

I have spoken of. If the policy of Mr. Lincoln and his Republican associates shall be carried out, or attempted to be carried out, no man in Georgia will be more willing or ready than myself to defend our rights, interest, and honor at every hazard and to the last extremity. What is this policy? It is, in the first place, to exclude us, by an act of Congress, from the Territories, with our slave property. He is for using the power of the General Government against the extension of our institutions. Our position on this point is, and ought to be, at all hazards, for perfect equality between all the States and the citizens of all the States in the Territories, under the Constitution of the United States. If Congress should exercise its power against this, then I am for standing where Georgia planted herself in 1850.[11] These were plain propositions which were there laid down in her celebrated platform as sufficient for the disruption of the Union if the occasion should ever come; on these Georgia has declared

---

11. A famous manifesto of the Georgia Convention of 1850, dominated by Unionists. After rejecting secession or any other "resistance" to the Compromise of 1850, the Convention declared that "Georgia will and ought to resist," and "even (as a last resort)," will and ought to secede, if (1). *Congress* abolished slavery in Washington D. C., or in any other place within the South (i.e. within a federal fort located in the South), or (2) *Congress* rejected a state's application to enter the Union because that state allowed slavery, or (3). *Congress* prohibited slavery in the Utah or New Mexican Territories or (4). *Congress* repealed or "materially" weakened the Federal Fugitive Slave Law of 1850. The Georgia Convention further declared its "deliberate opinion— that upon a faithful execution of the *Fugitive Slave Law* ... depends the preservation of our much beloved Union."

Note that this often-misunderstood Georgia Platform pledged "resistance" to *congressional* interference but not necessarily secession, except as "a last resort." Note further that the Georgia Platform did not pledge disunion or any other "resistance" if the *North* violated the Fugitive Slave Law; the platform only declared the "deliberate opinion" that the Union would not then last. This distinction between *pledging* resistance to *congressional* interference and *predicting* secession upon *northern* interference was critical, and Stephens, later in this speech, proposed to obliterate it. Georgia, he will be seen to argue, should pledge "resistance" and "even (as a last resort)" secession upon either *congressional* or *northern states'* interference with fugitive slave laws.

that she will go out of the Union, and for these she would be justified by the nations of the earth in so doing. I say the same; I said it then; I say it now, if Mr. Lincoln's policy should be carried out. I have told you that I do not think his bare election sufficient cause; but if his policy should be carried out, in violation of any of the principles set forth in the Georgia platform, that would be such an act of aggression, which ought to be met as therein provided for. If his policy shall be carried out in repealing or modifying the Fugitive Slave Law so as to weaken its efficacy, Georgia has declared that she will, in the last resort, disrupt the ties of the Union,—and I say so too. I stand upon the Georgia platform and upon every plank in it; and if these aggressions therein provided for take place, I say to you and to the people of Georgia, Be ready for the assault when it comes; keep your powder dry, and let your assailants then have lead, if need be. I would wait for an act of aggression. That is my position.

Now, upon another point, and that the most difficult and deserving your most serious consideration, I will speak. That is the course which this State should pursue toward those Northern States which, by their legislative acts, have attempted to nullify the Fugitive Slave Law. I know that in some of these States their acts, pretended to be based upon the principles set forth in the decision of the Supreme Court of the United States, in the case of Prigg against Pennsylvania; that decision did proclaim the doctrine that the State officers are not bound to carry out the provisions of a law of Congress; that the Federal Government cannot impose duties upon State officials; that they must execute their own laws by their own officers.[12] And this may be true. But still it is the duty of the

12. A critical United States Supreme Court decision of 1842, accurately described by Stephens.

States to deliver fugitive slaves, as well as it is the duty of the General Government to see that it is done.

The Northern States, on entering into the Federal compact, pledged themselves to surrender such fugitives; and it is in disregard of their constitutional obligations that they have passed laws which even tend to hinder or inhibit the fulfillment of that obligation. They have violated their plighted faith. What ought we to do in view of this? That is the question. What is to be done? By the law of nations you would have a right to demand the carrying out of this article of agreement, and I do not see that it should be otherwise with respect to the States of this Union; and in case it be not done, we would, by these principles, have the right to commit acts of reprisal on these faithless governments, and seize upon their property, or that of their citizens, wherever found. The States of this Union stand upon the same footing with foreign nations in this respect. But by the law of nations we are equally bound, before proceeding to violent measure, to set forth our grievances before the offending government, to give them an opportunity to redress the wrong. Has our State yet done this? I think not.

Suppose it were Great Britain that had violated some compact of agreement with the General Government, what would be first done? In that case our Minister would be directed in the first instance to bring the matter to the attention of that Government, or a commissioner be sent to that country to open negotiations with her, ask for redress, and it would only be after argument and reason had been exhausted in vain that we would take the last resort of nations. That would be the course toward a foreign Government; and toward a member of this Confederacy I would recommend the same course. Let us not, therefore, act hastily or ill-temperedly in this matter. Let your Committee on the state of the Republic make out a bill of grievances; let it be sent by the Governor to those faithless States; and if reason and argument shall be tried in vain,—if all shall fail to induce them to return to their constitutional obligations, I would be for retaliatory measures, such as the Governor has suggested to you.[13] This mode of resistance in the Union is in our power. It might be effectual; and in the last resort we would be justified in the eyes of nations, not only in separating from them, but in using force.

(*A voice.*—"The argument is already exhausted.")

Some friend says that the argument is already exhausted. No, my friend, it is not. You have never called the attention of the Legislatures of those States to this subject that I am aware of. Nothing on this line has ever been done before this year. The attention of our own people has been called to the subject lately.

Now, then, my recommendation to you would be this: In view of all these questions of difficulty, let a convention of the people of Georgia be called, to which they may all be referred. Let the sovereignty of the people speak. Some think that the election of Mr. Lincoln is cause sufficient to dissolve the Union. Some think those other grievances are sufficient to dissolve the same, and that the Legislature has the power thus to act, and ought thus to act. I have no hesitation in saying that the Legislature is not the proper body to sever our federal relations, if that necessity should arise. An honorable and distinguished gentleman, the other night (Mr. T. R. R. Cobb), advised you to take this course,—not to wait to hear from the cross-roads and groceries.

I say to you you have no power so to act. You must refer this question to the people, and you must wait to hear from the men at the cross-roads and even the groceries; for the people of this country, whether at the cross-roads or groceries, whether in cottages or palaces, are all equal, and they are the sovereigns in this country. Sovereignty is not in the Legislature. We, the

13. Stephens here referred to Joseph E. Brown's Special Message of November 7, 1860. See above, pp. xi–xii.

people, are sovereigns. I am one of them, and have a right to be heard; and so has every other citizen of the State. You legislators—I speak it respectfully—are but our servants. You are the servants of the people, and not their masters. Power resides with the people in this country. The great difference between our country and all others, such as France and England and Ireland, is, that here there is popular sovereignty, while there sovereignty is exercised by kings and favored classes. This principle of popular sovereignty, however much derided lately, is the foundation of our institutions. Constitutions are but the channels through which the popular will may be expressed. Our Constitution came from the people. They made it, and they alone can rightfully unmake it.

(**MR. TOOMBS.**—"I am afraid of conventions.")

I am not afraid of any convention legally chosen by the people. I know no way to decide great questions affecting fundamental laws except by representatives of the people. The Constitution of the United States was made by the representatives of the people in convention. The constitution of the State of Georgia was made by representatives of the people in convention, chosen at the ballot-box. Let us, therefore, now have a convention chosen by the people. But do not let the question which comes before the people be put to them in the language of my honorable friend who addressed you last night: "Will you submit to abolition rule or resist?"

(**MR. TOOMBS.**—"I do not wish the people to be cheated.")

Now, my friends, how are we going to cheat the people by calling on them to elect delegates to a convention to decide all these questions, without any dictation or direction? Who proposes to cheat the people by letting them speak their own untrammelled views in the choice of their ablest and best men, to determine upon all these matters involving their peace?

I think the proposition of my honorable friend had a considerable smack of unfairness, not to say cheat. He wishes to have no convention, but for the Legislature to submit this ques-

tion to the people, "submission to abolition rule or resistance."
Now, who in Georgia would vote "submission to abolition rule"?

Is putting such a question to the people to vote on a fair
way of getting an expression of the popular will on these questions? I think not. Now, who in Georgia is going to submit to
abolition rule?

(**MR. TOOMBS.**—"The convention will.")

No, my friend, Georgia will not do it. The convention will
not recede from the Georgia platform. Under that there can be
no abolition rule in the General Government. I am not afraid
to trust the people in convention upon this and all other questions. Besides, the Legislature was not elected for such a purpose. They came here to do their duty as legislators. They have
sworn to support the Constitution of the United States. They
did not come here to disrupt this Government. I am, therefore,
for submitting all these questions to a convention of the people.
To submit these questions to the people whether they would
submit to abolition rule or resist, and then for the Legislature
[not] to act on that vote, would be an insult to the people.

But how will it be under this arrangement if they should
vote to resist, and the Legislature should re-assemble with this
vote as their instructions? Can any man tell what sort of resistance will be meant? One man would, say, secede; another,
pass retaliatory measures,—these are measures of resistance
against wrong, legitimate and right,—and there would be as
many different ideas as there are members on this floor. Resistance don't mean secession,—that is no proper sense of the
term resistance. Believing that the times require action, I am
for presenting the question fairly to the people, for calling together an untrammelled convention, and presenting all the
questions to them whether they will go out of the Union, or
what course of resistance in the Union they may think best,
and then let the Legislature act, when the people in their majesty are heard, and I tell you now, whatever that convention
does, I hope and trust our people will abide by. I advise the

calling of a convention, with the earnest desire to preserve the peace and harmony of the State. I should dislike above all things to see violent measures adopted, or a disposition to take the sword in hand, by individuals, without the authority of law.

My honorable friend said last night, "I ask you to give me the sword; for if you do not give it to me, as God lives, I will take it myself."

(MR. TOOMBS.—"I will.")

I have no doubt that my honorable friend feels as he says. It is only his excessive ardor that makes him use such an expression; but this will pass off with the excitement of the hour. When the people in their majesty shall speak, I have no doubt he will bow to their will, whatever it may be upon the "sober second thought."

Should Georgia determine to go out of the Union, I speak for one, though my views might not agree with them, whatever the result may be, I shall bow to the will of the people. Their cause is my cause, and their destiny is my destiny, and I trust this will be the ultimate course of all. The greatest curse that can befall a free people is civil war.

But, as I said, let us call a convention of the people. Let all these matters be submitted to it, and when the will of a majority of the people has thus been expressed, the whole State will present one unanimous voice in favor of whatever may be demanded; for I believe in the power of the people to govern themselves, when wisdom prevails and passion does not control their actions. Look at what has already been done by them in their advancement in all that ennobles man! There is nothing like it in the history of the world. Look abroad from one extent of the country to the other; contemplate our greatness. We are now among the first nations of the earth. Shall it be said, then, that our institutions, founded upon the principles of self-government, are a failure?

Thus far, it is a noble example, worthy of imitation. The

gentleman (Mr. Cobb), the other night, said it had proven a failure. A failure in what? In growth? Look at our expanse in national power. Look at our population and increase in all that makes a people great. A failure! Why, we are the admiration of the civilized world, and present the brightest hopes of mankind.

Some of our public men have failed in their aspirations, that is true; and from that comes a great part of our troubles.

No; there is no failure of this Government yet. We have made great advancement under the Constitution, and I cannot but hope that we shall advance higher still. Let us be true to our trust.

Now, when this convention assembles, if it shall be called, as I hope it may, I would say, in my judgment, without dictation, for I am conferring with you freely and frankly, and it is thus that I give my views, it should take into consideration all those questions which distract the public mind; should view all the grounds of secession so far as the election of Mr. Lincoln is concerned; and I can but hope, if reason is unbiased by passion, that they would say that the constitutional election of no man is a sufficient cause to break up the Union, but that the State should wait until he at least does commit some unconstitutional act.

(**MR. TOOMBS.**—"Commit some overt act?")

No; I did not say that. The word *overt* is a sort of technical term connected with treason which has come to us from the mother-country, and it means an open act of rebellion. I do not see how Mr. Lincoln can do this unless he should levy war upon us. I do not, therefore, use the word *overt*. I do not intend to wait for that. But I use the word *unconstitutional act,* which our people understand much better, and which expresses just what I mean. But as long as he conforms to the Constitution he should be left to exercise the duties of his office.

In giving this advice, I am but sustaining the Constitution of my country, and I do not thereby become a "Lincoln aid man" either, but a constitutional aid man. But this matter the convention can determine.

As to the other matter, I think we have a right to pass retaliatory measures, provided they be in accordance with the Constitution of the United States; and I think they can be made so. But whether it would be wise for this Legislature to do this now is the question. To the convention, in my judgment, this matter ought to be referred. Before making reprisals, we should exhaust every means of bringing about a peaceful settlement of the controversy. Thus did General Jackson in the case of the French.[14] He did not recommend reprisals until he had treated with France and got her to promise to make indemnification, and it was only on her refusal to pay the money which she had promised that he recommended reprisals. It was after negotiation had failed. I do think, therefore, that it would be best, before going to extreme measures with our confederate States, to make the presentation of our demands, to appeal to their reason and judgment to give us our rights. Then, if reason should not triumph, it will be time enough to commit reprisals, and we should be justified in the eyes of a civilized world. At least let these offending and derelict States know what your grievances are, and if they refuse, as I said, to give us our rights under the Constitution, I should be willing, as a last resort, to sever the ties of our union with them.

My own opinion is, that if this course be pursued, and they are informed of the consequences of refusal, these States will recede, will repeal their nullifying acts; but if they should not, then let the consequences be with them, and the responsibility of the consequences rest upon them. Another thing I would have that convention do. Reaffirm the Georgia platform with an additional plank in it. Let that plank be the fulfillment of these constitutional obligations on the part of those States,—

14. Stephens here referred to President Andrew Jackson's handling of commercial/navigation disputes with France in the 1830s.

their repeal of these obnoxious laws as the condition of our remaining in the Union. Give them time to consider it; and I would ask all States South to do the same thing.

I am for exhausting all that patriotism demands before taking the last step. I would invite, therefore, South Carolina to a conference. I would ask the same of all the Southern States, so that if the evil has got beyond our control, which God in His mercy grant may not be the case, we may not be divided among ourselves; but, if possible, secure the united co-operation of all the Southern States, and then in the face of the civilized world we may justify our action, and with the wrong all on the other side, we can appeal to the God of battles, if it comes to that, to aid us in our cause. But do nothing in which any portion of our people may charge you with rash or hasty action. It is certainly a matter of great importance to tear this Government asunder. You were not sent here for that purpose. I would wish the whole South to be united if this is to be done; and I believe if we pursue the policy which I have vindicated, this can be effected.

In this way our sister Southern States can be induced to act with us; and I have but little doubt that the States of New York, Pennsylvania, Ohio, and the other Western States will compel their Legislatures to recede from their hostile attitude, if the others do not. Then, with these, we would go on without New England, if she chose to stay out.

(**A voice.**—"We will kick them out.")

No; I would not kick them out. But if they chose to stay out, they might. I think, moreover, that these Northern States, being principally engaged in manufactures, would find that they had as much interest in the Union under the Constitution as we, and that they would return to their constitutional duty,—this would be my hope. If they should not, and if the Middle States and Western States do not join us, we should at least have an undivided South. I am, as you clearly perceive, for maintaining the Union as it is, if possible. I will exhaust every means thus to maintain it with an equality in it.

My position, then, in conclusion, is for the maintenance of the honor, the rights, the equality, the security, and the glory of my native State in the Union if possible; but if these cannot be maintained in the Union, then I am for their maintenance, at all hazards, out of it. Next to the honor and glory of Georgia, the land of my birth, I hold the honor and glory of our common country. In Savannah I was made to say by the reporters, who very often make me say things which I never did, that I was first for the glory of the whole country and next for that of Georgia. I said the exact reverse of this. I am proud of her history, of her present standing. I am proud even of her motto, which I would have duly respected at the present time by all her sons,—"Wisdom, Justice, and Moderation." I would have her rights and those of the Southern States maintained now upon these principles. Her position now is just what it was in 1850, with respect to the Southern States. Her platform then established was subsequently adopted by most, if not all, the other Southern States. Now I would add but one additional plank to that platform, which I have stated, and one which time has shown to be necessary; and if that shall likewise be adopted in substance by all the Southern States, all may yet be well. But if all this fails, we shall at least have the satisfaction of knowing that we have done our duty and all that patriotism could require.

4

Benjamin H. Hill's Unionist Speech, Thursday Evening, November 15

In the late 1850s, Georgians considered Benjamin H. Hill to be Democrats' greatest opponent. The only non-Democrat among these debaters, he had gained special prominence when running, unsuccessfully, against the Democrats' Joseph Brown for the governorship in 1857. Hill, a sometimes state legislator, could carry his anti-Democratic Party rhetoric to an insulting extreme. In 1856, for example, an offended Stephens challenged Hill to a duel. Hill refused because, so he said, he had "a family to support and a soul to save," while Alexander Stephens had neither!

In the aftermath of Lincoln's election, Stephens for the first time joined Hill in opposition to most upper-class Democrats, who were mostly secessionists. But these two life-long foes' positions, vis-à-vis each other, would soon flip again. Hill would imminently become an advocate of the party in power, while Stephens would remain a proponent of the clique in opposition. Thus where Stephens, as Vice President of the Southern Confederacy, would oppose President Jefferson Davis, Hill, as a

Confederate Senator, would champion the President. After the war, Hill, at last a Democrat, would spend fifteen years as Georgia's very powerful United States Senator, while Stephens would become a rather inconsequential House member.

Those who heard Benjamin Hill on November 15, 1860 might have predicted that the Democrats' oft-beaten opponent would not lose forever. Following Stephens, after all, was an impossible assignment. Who could do better, with the same unionist argument? Well, Hill spoke almost as effectively, and won fame for it.[1]

Ladies and Friends: While I am speaking to you to-night I earnestly beg for perfect quietness and order. It seems to be a general idea that public speakers feel highly complimented when their opinions are received with boisterous applause. I do not so feel on any occasion, and certainly would not so regard such a demonstration now. The occasion is a solemn and serious one, and let us treat it in no light or trivial manner. One more request. I have invoked good order. I yet more earnestly invoke your kind and considerate attention. No people ever assembled to deliberate a graver issue. The government is the result of much toil, much blood, much anxiety, and much treasure. For nearly a century we have been accustomed to speak and boast of it as the best on earth. Wrapped up in it are the lives, the happiness, the interests, and the peace of thirty millions of freemen now living, and of unnumbered millions in the future.

---

1. In the absence of the needed modern biography, posterity must make do with E. Merton Coulter, "Alexander H. Stephens Challenges Benjamin H. Hill to a Duel," *Georgia Historical Quarterly,* 57 (1973):179–99; Haywood J. Pearce, Jr., *Benjamin H. Hill: Secession and Reconstruction* (Chicago, 1928); and Benjamin H. Hill, Jr., *Benjamin H. Hill of Georgia: His Life, Speeches and Writings* (Atlanta, 1893), from which we have transcribed Hill's speech (pp. 238–50).

Whether we shall now destroy that government or make another effort to preserve it and reform its abuses, is the question before us. Is that question not entitled to all the wisdom, the moderation, and the prudence we can command? Were you ever at sea in a storm? Then you know the sailor often finds it necessary, to enable him to keep his ship above the wave, to throw overboard his freight, even his treasure. But with his chart and his compass he never parts. However dark the heavens or furious the winds, with these he can still point the polar star, and find the port of his safety. Would not that sailor be mad who should throw these overboard?

We are at sea, my friends. The skies are fearfully darkened. The billows roll threateningly. Dangers are on every side. Let us throw overboard our passions, our prejudices, and our party feelings, however long or highly valued. But let us hold on— hold on to reason and moderation. These, and these alone, point always to the fixed star of truth, by whose guidance we may yet safely come to shore.

We must agree. We do agree if we but knew it. Our people must be united to meet this crisis. Divisions now would not only be unfortunate, but exceedingly disastrous. If divisions arise they cannot be based on our interests or our purposes, for these are and must be the same. Divisions must find their origin in our suspicions and jealousies. Let us give these suspicions and jealousies to the winds. Let us assume as the basis of every argument that we are all equally honest, and equally desirous in our various ways of securing one end—our equality and rights. There must be one way better than all others. Let our ambition be to find that way, and unite our people in the advocacy of that way.

I have listened with earnest attention to the eloquent speeches made by all sides, and I believe a common ground of agreement can be found, if not for universal, at least for very general agreement. Those who hold that the Constitution is wrong, and the Union bad *per se,* of course will agree to nothing but immediate disunion, and such I shall not be able to affect.

In the first place what are our grievances[?] All the speakers, thus far, even the most ultra, have admitted that the mere Constitutional election of any man is no ground for resistance. The mere election of Mr. Lincoln is on all sides admitted not to be [a] grievance. Our State would not be thrown on a false issue on this point.

We complain, in general terms, that the anti-slavery sentiment at the North has been made an element of political power.

In proof of this we make the following specifications:

1. That a large political party has been organized in the Northern States, the great common idea of which is to prohibit the extension of slavery by Congress, and hostility to slavery generally.

2. That this party has succeeded in getting the control of many of the Northern State Legislatures and have procured the passage of acts nullifying the fugitive slave law, encouraging the rescue of fugitives, and seeking to punish as felons citizens of our Southern States who pursue their slaves in the assertion of a plain Constitutional right.

3. That this party has elected governors in Northern States who refuse, some openly and others under frivolous pretexts, to do their plain Constitutional duties, when these involve the recognition of property in slaves.

4. That Northern courts, chosen by the same party, have assumed to declare the fugitive slave law unconstitutional in the teeth of the decisions of the United States courts, and of every department of the United States Government.

5. We complain that the Northern States, thus controlled, are seeking to repudiate every Constitutional duty or provision, in favor or in recognition of slavery—to work the extinction of slavery, and to secure to the negro social and political equality

with the white race; and, as far as possible, they disregard
and nullify even the laws of the Southern States on these subjects. In proof of this complaint, we show that Northern governors have actually refused to deliver up fugitives from justice, when the crime charged against such fugitives [is flight
from a condition] recognized under State law [as] property
in slaves.

Thus, a Northern man married a Southern lady having a
separate estate in slaves. He deceived the lady, stole her negroes, sold them, and pocketed the money, and fled to a Northern State. He was charged with larceny under the laws of the
State in which the crime was committed. A true bill was obtained and a demand was properly made for his return, and
the Governor of the State to which he fled refused to deliver
him up on the ground that to commit larceny a man must steal
property, and as slaves were not property according to the laws
of the Northern State, it could not be property according to the
laws of the Southern State; that therefore the Southern court,
jury, and governor were all wrong in obeying the laws of their
own State, instead of the laws of the Northern State; that the
defendant was not guilty and could not be guilty, and should
not be delivered up.

The same principle was involved to shield several of the
conspirators in the John Brown raid.

The inexorable logic of this party, on such a premise, must
array them against the whole Constitution of the United
States; because that instrument, in its very frame-work, is a
recognition of property in slaves. It was made by slaveholding
States. Accordingly we find this party a disunion party, and
its leaders—those of them who follow their logic to its practical
consequences—disunionists *per se*. I would not quote from the
low and the ignorant of that party, but I will quote from the
learned and the honored.

One of the most learned disciples of this party, says:

The Constitution is the cause of every division which this vexed question of slavery has ever occasioned in this country. If (the Constitution) has been the fountain and father of our troubles, by attempting to hold together, as reconciled, two opposing principles, which will not harmonize nor agree, the only hope of the slave is over the ruins of the government [and of the American Church.] The dissolution of the Union is the abolition of slavery.[2]

One of the ablest, and oldest, and long honored senators of that party—a senator even before the existence of the Republican party—said to the nominating convention of that party:

I believe that this is not so much a convention to change the administration of the government, as to say whether there shall be any government to be administered. You have assembled, not to say whether this Union shall be preserved, but to say whether it shall be a blessing or a scorn and hissing among the nations.[3]

I could quote all night, my friends, to show that the tendency of the Republican party is to disunion. That to be a Republican is to be logically and practically against the Constitution and the Union. And we complain that this party is warring upon us, and at the same time, and in the same way, and by a necessary consequence, warring upon the Constitution and the Union.

6. We complain, in the last place, that this party, having

2. Hill here quoted the Reverend Henry Ward Beecher's speech in New Haven, Connecticut in 1856. Hill omitted part of one Beecher sentence, which we have restored in brackets.

3. Hill here quoted New Hampshire's John P. Hale, addressing the Republican National Convention on June 17, 1856.

thus acquired the control of every department of government—legislative, executive, and judicial—in several of the Northern States, and having thus used every department of the State government so acquired, in violation of the Constitution of the United States, in disregard of the laws of the Southern States, and in utter denial of the property and even liberty of the citizens of the Southern States—this party, I say, with these principles, and this history, has at last secured the executive department of the Federal Government, and are seeking to secure the other two departments—the legislative and the judicial.

Here, then, is a party seeking to administer the government on principles which must destroy the government—proposing to preserve the Union upon a basis on which the Union, in the very nature of things, cannot stand; and offering peace on terms which must produce civil war.

Now, my friends, the next question is, shall these grievances be resisted? I know of no man who says they ought not to be resisted. For myself, I say, and say with emphasis, they ought to be resisted—resisted effectively and at all hazards.

What lessons have we here? We have seen differences running high—even apparent bitterness engendered. Passion gets up, debates become jeers and gibes and defiance. One man says he will not resist Lincoln. His adversary pronounces that treason to the South and the man a black Republican. Another man says he will resist Lincoln and demand immediate secession. His adversary pronounces that treason to the Constitution and the man a disunionist.

What do you mean by Lincoln? Stop and define. The first means by Lincoln the man elected, the second means by Lincoln the issue on which he is elected. Neither will resist the first, both will resist the latter, and so they agree and did agree all the time they were disputing!

These grievances are our real complaint. They have advanced to a point which makes a crisis: and that point is the

election of Lincoln. We dare not, we will not let this crisis pass
without a settlement. That settlement must wipe out existing
grievances, and arrest threatened ones. We owe it to our Constitution, to our country, to our peace, to our posterity, to our
dignity, to our self-respect as Union men and Southern men,
to have a cessation of these aggressions and an end to these
disturbances. I do not think we should wait for any further
violation of the Constitution. The Constitution has already
been violated and even defied. These violations are repeated
every day. We must resist, and to attempt to resist and not do
so effectively—even to the full extent of the evil—will be to
bring shame on ourselves, and our State, and our cause.

Having agreed on our complaints, and discovered that all
our suspicions of each other are unfounded, and that our disputes on this point had their origin in hasty conclusions and
thoughtless mistakes, let us, with an encouraged charity and
forbearance, advance to the next step in this argument.

Who shall inaugurate this resistance? Who shall determine the mode, the measure, and the time of this resistance?

My reply is: The people through their delegate convention
duly assembled.

It is not necessary for me now to urge this point. Here
again we have had disputes without differences.

I have the pleasure of announcing to-night that the prominent leaders, of all shades of opinion on this subject, came
together this day, and agreed that it was the right and privilege
of the people in convention to pass on these questions.[4] On this
point we have disputed for a week, and to-day, acting as Georgians should act, we came together in a spirit of kindness, and
in fifteen minutes our hearts were all made glad by the dis-
covery that our differences or disputes were founded on ground-
less suspicions, and *we are agreed.* We are all for resistance,

4. For the context of Hill's remarks here, see above, pp. xvii–xviii.

and we are all for the people in convention to say how and where and by what means we shall resist.

I never beheld a scene which made my heart rejoice more sincerely. Oh, that I could see the same spirit of concord on the only remaining question of difference. With my heart full of kindness I beg you, my friends, accompany me now to question. I do believe we can agree again. My solemn conviction is that we differ as little on this as we did on the other point, in every material view. At least, nearly all the quarrels of the world in all ages have been founded more in form than substance.

Some men are honest, wise, and prudent. Others are equally honest and intelligent, but rash and impetuous. The latter are often to be loved and encouraged; but the first alone are to be relied on in emergencies.

We often appeal to the history of our fathers to urge men to indignation and resentment of wrongs. Let us study all that history. Let me show you from that history, an example of metal and over-confidence on the one hand, and of coolness and wisdom on the other.

During our colonial history, the English government sent General Braddock to America to dislodge and drive back the French and Indians.[5] The general, in arranging the company, assigned to his own command the duty of recovering the Ohio Valley and the great Northwest. It was necessary to capture Fort Duquesne. He never thought of any difficulties in the way of success. He promised Newcastle to be beyond the mountains in a very short period. [Fort] Duquesne he thought would stop

---

5. In July, 1755, a combined force of French and Indians ambushed and killed British General Edward Braddock at Fort Necessity, a crude fort located in Great Meadows, Pennsylvania. The ambush site was a few miles south of Fort Duquesne (itself located in the vicinity of present-day Pittsburgh), which Braddock had hoped to capture and then use to mount an invasion past the Alleghenies and on to the Niagara River. Braddock's debacle at Fort Necessity helped lead his English superiors, including Newcastle, to initiate the Seven Years War with France, 1756–63.

him only three or four days, and there was no obstruction to his march to Niagara. He declared the Indians might frighten the raw American militia, but could make no impression on the British regulars. This was Braddock.

One of that raw American militia who had joined Braddock's command, was the young Washington,[6] then only about twenty-three years old. He became one of Braddock's aids. Hearing his general's boasts, and seeing his thoughtless courage, Washington quietly said to him, "We shall have more to do than to go up the hills and come down." Speaking of Braddock to another, Washington said, "He was incapable of arguing without warmth, or giving up any point he had asserted, be it ever so incompatible with reason or common sense."

Braddock was considered on all hands to be a brave, gallant, and fearless officer.

Here, then, are two men, both brave, noble, and intelligent, engaged together to accomplish a common enterprise for the good of their country. The one was rash, thoughtless, never calculating difficulties, nor looking forward to and providing against obstructions.

He arranged his express and sent forward the news of his victory beforehand. But the other was cool, calculating, cautious, wise, and moderate. He was a man who thought before he acted and then he acted the hero.

Now, for results: Braddock was surprised before he reached the fort. His British regulars fled before the yelling Indians, and the raw American militia were slain by them. Braddock himself fought bravely and he was borne from the field of his shame, leaving more than half his little army dead, and himself senseless with a mortal wound. After the lapse of a day he came to himself, and his first exclamation was, "Who would have

---

6. Of course Hill here referred to George Washington. Most historians would say that Hill overpraised Washington, for the future President had himself been ambushed and driven away from Fort Necessity a year earlier.

thought it!" Again he roused up and said, "We shall better know how to deal with them another time." Poor general, it was too late, for with that sentence he died? For more than a century he has slept near Fort Necessity, and his only history might be written for his epitaph: "He was brave but rash, gallant but thoughtless, noble but bigoted. He fought hastily, died early, and here he lies."

The young Washington was also brave, and in the thickest of the fight. Horse after horse fell from under him. The bullets of the Indians whistled around him and through his clothes, but Providence spared him. Even the Indians declared some God protected him. So cool, so brave, so wise and thoughtful was the conduct of this young officer, before, during, and after the battle that even then a distinguished man "points him out as a youth raised up by Providence for some noble work." Who does not know the history of Washington; yet who can tell it? Our glorious revolution, that wise Constitution, this happy, widespread, and ever spreading country—struggling millions fired on by the example of his success, are some of the chapters already written in that history. Long chapters of yet unrealized glory, and power, and happiness shall be endlessly added, if the wisdom of him who redeemed our country can be continued to those who inherit it. The last hour of constitutional liberty, perpetuated to the glory of the end, or cut short in the frenzy of anarchy, shall wind up the history of Washington. Behold here the sudden destruction of the rash man and his followers, and the still unfolding success of the cool and thoughtful man, and then let us go to work to meet this crisis that is upon us.

Though there are various modifications of opinions, there are really but two modes of resistance proposed. One method is to make no further effort in the Union, but to assume that the Union either cannot or ought not to be preserved, and secede at once and throw ourselves upon the consequences. The other method is to exhaust certain remedies for these grievances in the Union, with the view of preserving our rights and the Union with them, if possible; looking, however, to and preparing for secession as an ultimate resort, certainly to be had, if those grievances cannot be remedied and completely remedied and ended in the Union.

Irreconcilable as these differences at first view seem to be, I maintain a point of complete reconciliation can be reached.

Now, let us look to the reason urged by the advocates of these two modes of redress.

The advocates of the first mode declare that these grievances are the fruits of an original, innate anti-slavery fanaticism. That the history of the world will show that such fanaticism is never convinced, is never satisfied, never reasons, and never ends but in victory or blood. That accordingly this fanaticism in the Northern States has been constantly progressive, always getting stronger and more impudent, defiant, and aggressive; and that it will never cease except in our subjugation unless we tear loose from it by dissolving the Union. These advocates say they have no faith in any resistance in the Union, because, in the nature of the evil, none can be effectual.

The advocates of the second mode of resistance, of whom I am humbly one, reason after another fashion: We say, in the first place, that while it is true that this anti-slavery sentiment has become fanatical with many, yet it is not necessarily so in its nature, nor was it so in its origin. Slavery has always existed in some form. It is an original institution. Besides, we say the agitation now upon us did not originate in fanaticism or philanthropy but in cupidity.

England owned the West Indies and there she had some slaves. She had possessions in East India which she believed were adapted to the growth of cotton, and which article of produce she desired to monopolize.

The Southern States were her only dangerous competitors. She desired to cripple or break down the cultivation of the cotton plant in the South. The South could not use her own soil and climate in the successful production of cotton without the African slave. England therefore must manage to set free the slave and turn the South over to some inadequate peasantry system, something like the coolie system. To this end England raised a great cry of philanthropy in behalf of the poor negro. As a show of sincerity she abolished slavery in the West Indies near us, thinking thereby to affect the same institutions in her Southern neighbor. She taught her lessons of false philanthropy to our Northern pulpits and Northern papers, and thus to our Northern people.

At this time the Northern politicians saw in this inflammable subject fine material for political agitation, party success, and self-promotion. They leaped upon the wave and rode on it. The Southern politicians raised the counter cry, leaped on the counter wave, and met the Northern politicians—in office. As long as the people answered the politicians called, and the result is what we now see. The subject is interminable in politics, because utterly illegitimate as a political issue. Thus it has never approached, but receded from a political solution, and increasing in excitement as it has progressed; all statesmanship, North and South, is dwarfed to a mere wrangling about African slavery. Slavery will survive, but the Constitution, the Union, and peace may not. The Southern States will continue to raise cotton, but the hoping subject of tyranny in the earth may not continue to point to the beautiful success of the experiment of self-government in America.

While the storm which England raised in America has been going on, England has been trying to raise cotton in India. She has failed. Her factories are at home, but her cotton can't come from India. She must have cotton. Four millions of her people can't live without it. The English throne can't stand without it. It must come from the Southern States. It can't be raised in the South without slave labor. And England has become the defender of slavery in the South.

I will frankly state that this revolution in English sentiment and policy has not yet reached the Northern people. The same causes must slowly produce it.

But while the anti-slavery sentiment has spread in the North, the pro-slavery sentiment has also strengthened in America. In our early history the Southern statesmen were anti-slavery in feeling. So were Washington, Jefferson, Madison, Randolph,[7] and many of that day, who had never studied the argument of the cotton gin, nor heard the eloquent productions of the great Mississippi Valley. Now our people not only see the justice of slavery, but its providence too. The world can never give up slavery until it is ready to give up clothing and food. The South is a magnificent exemplification of the highest Christian excellence. She is feeding the hungry, clothing the naked, blessing them that curse her, and doing good to them that despitefully use and persecute her.

We say again that even the history of the slavery agitation in this country does not justify the very conclusion that Abolitionism has been always progressive. Whenever popular sentiment in politics has condemned the agitation, Abolitionism has declined. Many instances could be given. In 1848 the Abolition candidate for the Presidency received about 300,000 votes. At the end of Mr. Fillmore's administration in 1852, the candidate of that party received about half that vote,[8] and a fugitive slave could be recovered almost without opposition in any Northern State. Even the act of Massachusetts, nullifying the fugitive slave law of 1703, had not been applied to the new fugitive slave law of 1850, and was not so applied until 1855, after the agitation had been revived.

These, and many other similar reasons, we urge for be-

7. Virginia' archconservative John Randolph of Roanoke, who, like George Washington, freed his slaves in his last will and testament.
8. The Free Soil candidate of 1848, New York's Martin Van Buren, almost doubled the vote of the party's 1852 candidate, New Hampshire's John P. Hale.

lieving that all the enumerated grievances—the results of slavery agitation—are curable by remedies within the Union.

But suppose our reasoning all wrong! How shall we be convinced? Only by the experiment; for in the nature of the case, nothing but a trial can test the virtue of the remedies proposed. Let us try these remedies, and if we fail, this failure will establish the truth of the positions of the advocates of immediate secession, and we shall all join in that remedy.

For let it be understood, we are all agreed that these grievances shall be resisted—shall be remedied—most effectively remedied; and if this cannot be done in the Union, then the Union must go. And we must not let this crisis pass without forever solving this doubt. If the Union and the peace of slavery cannot exist together, then the Union must go; for slavery can never go, the necessities of man and the laws of Heaven will never let it go, and it must have peace. And it has been tantalized and meddled with as long as our self-respect can permit.

But what remedies in the Union do we propose? I will answer:

The grievances enumerated are of two kinds—existing and threatened. The existing actual grievances are all violations of the Federal Constitution and Federal laws, either by Northern citizens or Northern States. Now, what does good statesmanship, good logic, and common sense naturally suggest? Why, that the Federal Government shall enforce its laws. No State can enforce, or punish, for the violation of a Federal law. The power offended must adequately punish the offender. The punishment must be such as to redress the past, and by certainty and terror secure the future. The Federal law is offended. The Northern States and people are the offenders. The South is damaged by the offense. This gives her the right to demand the redress at the hands of the Federal Government, and if that government, for want of will or power, shall not grant the redress, then that government is a demonstrated failure. And when government ends, self-defense begins. We can then take redress in our own way, and to our entire satisfaction.

Let the Georgia Convention meet. Let her not simply demand but command that this war on slavery shall cease—that these unconstitutional acts and proceeding shall be repealed and abandoned by the States, or repudiated and redressed by the Federal Government.[9] Let her invite all the [Northern and Southern] States to join in this demand. If no others will come to their duty and meet with us, let the fifteen Southern States join in this demand, and let the penalty of refusal, even to the demand of one State, be the abandonment of the Union, and any other, even harsher remedy, each State may think her rights and honor require.

We have an instance before us, made by the North. When, in 1833, South Carolina was refusing to obey a Federal law, in the execution of which the Northern States had an interest, Congress passed a force bill, and put it in the hands of a Southern President for enforcement, even with the army and the navy and the militia—if needed.[10]

Let us turn this battery against Northern rebels. The constitutionality of the act which South Carolina resisted was doubted. A Southern State never nullified, nor refused to obey, a plain constitutional law. But here are the Northern States, and people nullifying and setting at defiance the plainest Constitutional provisions, and laws passed in pursuance thereof; and, instead of demanding of the Federal Government the en-

---

9. Again, the northern Personal Liberty Laws, making enforcement of the federal Fugitive Slave Law more difficult.

10. The Force Bill of 1833 gave President Andrew Jackson of Tennessee greater authority to enforce tariff laws against the South Carolina nullifiers. The Compromise Tariff of 1833 ended the Nullification Crisis before Jackson needed to use the Force Bill. South Carolinians, when agreeing to the new tariff, pleased themselves by declaring the now unnecessary Force Bill null and void.

forcement of its laws for the protection of our rights, we are
spending our breath and wasting our strength, in vain boast-
ings of wrath and hurtful divisions of our own people.

Some of our wisest Southern statesmen think we have laws
already sufficient for this crisis, if enforced. We have an act in
1795, and one in 1807, and perhaps others, to execute the laws,
to suppress insurrections, and repel invasions. If these and
other enactments are sufficient, let us have them enforced.

A Voice.—The presidents we have already had won't enforce that law.

Mr. Hill.—Then you ought to have dissolved long ago. If
the grievance has been by men of our own choosing, why have
we not complained before[?] Let us begin now. Let us begin
with Mr. Buchanan. A few days ago, and perhaps now, a fugitive is standing protected by a Northern mob in a Northern
State, in defiance of the United States Marshal. Let us demand
now that Mr. Buchanan enforce the law against that rebel and
against that State which protects him, or suffers him to be
protected on her soil. Let us have out the army and navy, and
if they are not sufficient let there be a call for volunteers. Many
of us say we are ready to fight, anxious to fight. Here is a chance.
Let us tender our services.

If the laws now existing are not sufficient, let us have them
sufficient. It is our right. We are entitled to a force bill for every
clause in the Constitution necessary to our rights. What have
our statesmen been after that these laws are not sufficient?
Some of these nullifying grievances have existed since 1843,
and is it possible that our statesmen have been all asleep, or
lost or forgetful in wrangling about slavery? Let us begin now
and perfect our laws for the enforcement of every Constitutional right, and against every rebel enemy. Let the convention
add to the contingencies of disruption in the Georgia platform.[11]

---

11. Hill here echoed, and Herschel V. Johnson would the next day reecho,
Alexander Stephens's call for an expanded Georgia Platform. See above, p. 69.

Let the refusal to enforce the laws granted for our protection and defense be one contingency, and the refusal to grant the laws needed for that protection and defense be another contingency.

A Voice.—How long will you wait?

Mr. Hill.—Until the experiment is tried and both the demands enumerated may be tested and the contingencies may transpire before the fourth of March next. If they do not, if a larger time shall be needed, Mr. Lincoln cannot do us damage. As you heard last night, he cannot even form his Cabinet unless he make it acceptable to a Democratic Senate. And I go further and say that he cannot get even his salary—not a dime to pay for his breakfast—without the consent of Congress.

Nor would I have the Southern States, nor even Georgia, to hesitate to demand the enforcement of those laws at the hands of Mr. Lincoln, if we cannot test it before. The North demanded of a Southern President the execution of the law against a Southern State in 1833. Now let the South compel a Northern President to execute the laws against a Northern people; yea, the very rebels that elected him.

A Voice.—Do you believe Lincoln would issue his proclamation?

Mr. Hill.—We can make him do it. It is his oath. He will be a traitor to refuse, and we shall have the right to hang him. He dare not refuse. He would be on Southern territory, and for his life he dare not refuse.

A Voice.—The "Wide Awakes" will be there.[12]

Mr. Hill.—Very well, if we are afraid of the "Wide Awakes" we had better surrender without further debate. The "Wide Awakes" will be there if we secede, and if they are to be dreaded, our only remedy is to hide. No, my friends, we are not afraid

12. The name used by Republican marching clubs in the campaign of 1860. These youthful partisan parading groups had a martial air, with their oilcloth capes, glazed hats, and lighted torches.

of anybody. Arm us with the laws of our country and the Constitution of our fathers, and we fear no enemy. Let us make
war upon that Constitution and against those laws and we will
be afraid of every noise in the bushes. He who feels and knows
he is right, is afraid of nothing; and he who feels and knows
he is wrong, is afraid of nothing, too.

We were told the other night by a gentleman urging immediate secession that we had never had a member in Congress
but who was afraid to demand the laws for the enforcement of
these Constitutional rights. And this is true, but whose fault
is that? Shame upon us that we have been afraid to demand
our rights at the hands of our own government, administered
to this hour by men of our own choice, and yet insist on our
courage to sustain us in seceding from that government in
defiance of its power. No, we have a right to go out, but let us
know we *must* exercise that right before we go, and how can
we know it unless we ask first? The Declaration of Independence, which you invoke for an example, says, a decent respect
to the opinions of mankind requires us to declare the causes
which impel us to the separation. When we separate and allege
our grievances as our causes, and mankind shall ask us if we
attempted, even demanded a redress of those grievances and
causes before we went out, shall we hang our heads and say
no? A people who are afraid to demand respect for their rights,
can have no rights worthy to be respected. Our fathers demanded, yea petitioned, warned, and conjured, and not until
the government was deaf to the voice of justice and consan-
guinity, did they acquiesce in the necessity which announced
their separation. It is not the cowardice of fear, but the courage
of right and duty, to demand redress at the hands of our
government.

I confess I am anxious to see the strength of this government now tested. The crisis is on us; not of our seeking, but in
spite of our opposition, and now let us meet it.

I believe we can make Lincoln enforce the laws. If fifteen

Southern States will take that Constitution and the laws and his oath, and shake them in the face of the President, and demand their observance and enforcement, he cannot refuse. Better make *him* do it than any one else. It will be a magnificent vindication of the power and the majesty of the law, to make the President enforce the law, even to hanging, against the very rebels who have chosen him to trample upon it. It will be a vindication that will strike terror to the hearts of the evil-doers for a century to come. Why, Lincoln is not a monarch. He has no power outside of the law, and none inside of the law except to enforce it. The law is our king over all. From the President to the humblest citizen we are the equal subjects of this only ruler. We have no cause for fear except when we offend this only sovereign of the Republican citizen, and have no occasion for despair until his protection is denied us.

I am also willing, as you heard last night, that our Convention or State should demand of the nullifying States the repeal of their obnoxious laws. I know this idea has been characterized as ridiculous. I cannot see wherein. You would make such demands of any foreign power interfering with your rights, and why do less toward a confederate State?

But in my opinion, the wisest policy, the most natural remedy, and the surest way to vindicate our honor and self-respect, is to demand the unconditional observance of the Constitution by every State and people, and to enforce that demand. And if it be necessary, call out for this purpose the whole power of the government even to war on the rebellious State. And when a State shall allow a fugitive to be rescued in her jurisdiction and carried beyond the reach of the owner, require her to indemnify the owner, and make the government compel that indemnity, even to the seizure of the property of the offending State and her people. One such rigid enforcement of the law will secure universal obedience. Let the law be executed though the heavens fall, for there can be no government without law, and law is but sand, if not enforced. If need be, let the State

continuing in rebellion against the Constitution be driven from
the Union. Is this Union a good? If so, why should we surrender
its blessings because Massachusetts violates the laws of that
Union? Punish the guilty. Drive Massachusetts to the duties
of the Constitution or from its benefits. Make the general government do this, and abandon the government when it shall
take sides with the criminal. It would be a trophy to fanaticism,
above all her insolence, to drive the dutiful out of the Union
with impunity on its part. Let us defend the Union against its
enemies, until that Union shall take sides with the enemy, and
then let us defend ourselves against both.

In the next place let us consider the benefits of this policy.
First, let us consider its benefits if we succeed; and then its
benefits if we fail.

If we succeed we shall have brought about a triumph of
law over the fell spirit of mobocracy, never surpassed in the
world's history, and the reward of that triumph will be the
glorious vindication of our equality and honor, and at the same
time the establishment of the Union in its integrity forever.
And I tell you, my friends, we owe it to our history, ourselves,
and our posterity, yea, to constitutional liberty itself, to make
this trial. Can it be possible that we are living under a government that has no power to enforce its laws? We have boasted
of our form of government. We have almost canonized its au-
thors as saints, for their patriotism and wisdom. They have
reputations world-wide. They have been, for nearly a century
lauded as far above all antiquity, and all previous statesmen.
Their face and their forms have been perpetuated in brass and
marble for the admiring gaze of many generations made happy
in the enjoyment of their labors. In verse and song, in history
and philosophy, in light literature and grave learning, their
names are eulogized, and their deeds commemorated, and their
wisdom ennobled. The painter has given us the very faces and
positions of the great counselors, as they sat together delib-
erating in the formation of this Constitution. The pulpit has

placed their virtues next to the purity and inspiration of the early apostles. The Senate Chamber has invoked their sayings as the test of good policy. The fireside has held up to its juvenile circle their manners as the models of good breeding. The demagogue on the hustings has falsely caught at their mantles to hide his own shame.

All this, because we have been accustomed to believe that they succeeded in framing the best Constitution and in organizing the best government the world ever saw. Is that government, after all, a failure? Who shall give us a better, and how shall we commemorate the worth of such wiser benefactors? But if this government cannot enforce its laws, then it is a failure.

We have professed to feel and realize its blessings. Eloquence has portrayed in magic power its progress in all the elements of power, wealth, greatness, and happiness. Not a people on earth, since we achieved our independence, has shown symptoms of a desire to be free, that we have not encouraged by our sympathies, and as the sufficient evidence of all success in self-government, we have pointed them to our example. There is not a people on earth who do not point to America and sigh for a government like that of the United States. Shall we now say to all these: Stop, you are mistaken. Our reputation is not deserved. Be content with your harsher rule. The people are not capable of self-government. This very government, which you admire, and which we have thought was a model is unable to protect our own people from the robber, the thief, the murderer and the fanatic!

Fellow-citizens, before we settle down in such a conclusion, let us make the effort and put this government to the test.

Another advantage to be derived from success is, that we shall thus end the agitation of slavery forever. Its agitation in politics was wrong from the beginning. Debate its morality and justice as much as you please. It will stand the argument. But don't drag it down into a party political issue. Show me the

man who agitates slavery as a political party question and I
will show you the true enemy of slavery and the Union, I care
not whether he lives North or South. The safety and peace of
the slaveholder and the Union demand that this agitation
should not longer be allowed.

But, in the second place, if we fail, we cannot be damaged,
but great benefits will result from the effort.

In the next place we shall have time to get ready for secession. If we secede now, in what condition are we? Our secession
will either be peaceable or otherwise. If peaceable, we have no
ships to take off our produce. We could not get and would not
have those of the government from which we had just seceded.
We have no treaties, commercial or otherwise, with any other
power. We have no postal system among our own people. Nor
are we prepared to meet any one of the hundred inconveniences
that must follow, and all of which can be avoided by taking
time.

But suppose our secession be not peaceable. In what condition are we for war? No navy, no forts, no arsenals, no arms
but bird guns for low trees. Yet a scattered people, with nothing
dividing us from our enemy but an imaginary line, and a long
sea and gulf cc ist extending from the Potomac to Galveston
Bay, if all should secede. In what condition are we to meet the
thousand ills that would beset us, and every one of which can
be avoided by taking time. "We have more to do than to go up
the hills and come down."[13] Secession is no holiday work.

While we are seeking to redress our wrongs in the Union,
we can go forward, making all necessary preparations to go
out if it should become necessary. We can have a government
system perfect, and prepared, ready for the emergency, when
the necessity for separation shall come.

Again, if we fail to get redress in the Union, that very

13. Hill here referred back to his quote from George Washington, addressing Edward Braddock. See above, p. 88.

failure will unite the people of our State. The only real ground of difference now is: some of us think we can get redress in the Union, and others think we cannot. Let those of us who still have faith make that effort which has never been made, and if we fail, then we are ready to join you. If you will not help us make that effort, at least do not try to prevent [it]. Let us have a fair trial. Keep cool and keep still. If we cannot save our equality, and rights, and honor in the Union, we shall join you and save them out of it.

Voice.—When you fail to save your rights in the Union, if you refuse to go with us then, what will you do?

Mr. Hill.—But we will go. We allow not *if* to our conduct in that connection. If, when we come to join you, you get stubborn and refuse to go, then we shall go without you.

Now, my secession friends, I have all confidence in your zeal and patriotism, but simply let us take time and get ready. Let us work for the best, and prepare for the worst. Until an experiment is made, I shall always believe that the Constitution has strength enough to conquer all its enemies—even the Northern fanatic. If it proves to have not that strength, I will not trust it another hour.

A third benefit to be derived from the failure of an honest effort to redress our grievances in the Union, is the Union of all the Southern States. Some of the States will not secede now. Some of the States who suffer most from the grievances we have enumerated will not secede now. Because they think these grievances can be redressed in the Union. If this idea be a dream, let us wake up to the reality by an actual experiment.

A further benefit to be desired is, that if all the Southern States get ready and secede together, we shall be allowed to do so peaceably. Certainly, it is our right to go peaceably any way. The government, though having the right to enforce its laws against all the world, has no right to coerce back a seceding State. But the attempt might be made and the peace broken, if only one State should secede, or even a few. But let all the

Southern States get ready and go together, and no earthly power would interfere or molest. My own opinion is that every Western and Northwestern State, and the Middle States, and perhaps all but the New England States, would go with us. And the glorious result at last might be that we should hold the government with all its power, and thrust off only those who have been faithless to it.

But the Southern States alone, with the territory naturally falling into our hands, would form the greatest government then on earth. The world must have our products; and after peace was once secured to us, the world would furnish our navies and our army, without the expense to us of a ship or a soldier.

Finally, my friends, we shall have secured, by this policy, the good opinion of all mankind and of ourselves. We shall have done our duty to history, to our children, and to Constitutional liberty, the great experiment of self-government. We shall have also discerned the defects in our present government, and will be prepared to guard against them in another. Above all we shall have found good consciences, and secured that, either in the Union or out of it, which is dearer to us than any Union, and more to be desired than all constitutions however venerated—that which is the end of all our efforts, and the desire of all our hearts, our equality as States, our rights as citizens, and our honor as men.

5

Herschel V. Johnson's Unionist Public Letter, Friday, November 16, from Milledgeville

Herschel V. Johnson, not nearly as prominent in the history books as Toombs or Stephens, loomed almost as large in antebellum years. Johnson was a huge man, over 245 pounds. He was also very wealthy, as his showpiece of a plantation, "Sandy Grove," demonstrated. He was, moreover, large in political accomplishment, having served during the 1850s as United States Senator, governor, and judge.

But Herschel Johnson lost too often to match the power of the more persistent winners. In 1850–51, Johnson advocated resistance, short of secession, to the Compromise of 1850. The Toombs-Stephens-Cobb unionist triumvirate routed Johnson's States' Rights Party. So too in 1860, Johnson was the Vice Presidential candidate on Stephen A. Douglas's ticket. The Douglas candidacy was demolished in the South. When he wrote the following unionist public letter of November 16, 1860, Johnson, unknowingly, lined up on the losing side again.

Johnson's letter from Milledgeville reads more like a winner's dispatch. Coming on the heels of Stephen's and Hill's or-

ations, Johnson's missive was another cogent plea for safer resistances than secession. Johnson particularly insisted that his alternatives of 1850, then irresponsibly rejected, must now be expanded and responsibly tried out, before a civil war should be risked.[1]

Gentlemen:—I am in receipt of your note of yesterday requesting me to deliver an address upon the "perilous issue now upon the country." After mature reflection, I decline to comply with your request. Several able speeches have been made, during the week, on both sides and I could not hope to add a single ray to the flood of light which has been poured upon the great questions which are before the Legislature and engage the minds of the people. As a substitute for a speech, I offer you the following brief expression of my views:

Much as I deplore the election of Lincoln, it is an event which I confidently expected, from the moment of the disruption of the Chat'n [Charleston] Convention.[2] It requires all the energies of a united Democracy to elect a President; with a divided Democracy, it is impossible. To that schism therefore, must be ascribed our defeat. If the Convention had harmoniously nominated any distinguished Democrat, either North or South, upon the Cincinnati platform, with the Dred Scott Decision, I

1. The best biography is Percy Scott Flippin, *Herschel V. Johnson of Georgia: States Rights Unionist* (Richmond, 1931). We have transcribed Johnson's public letter from *The* (Milledgeville Weekly) *Southern Recorder,* November 27, 1860.

2. Johnson here referred to the breakup of the Democratic Party in 1860. See Chapter 3, note 2, p. 55. Note that Johnson, like Stephens, thought that the Lower South had erred in Charleston and thus brought on its own misfortune: Lincoln's election.

believe he would have been elected.[3] But in the election of General Pierce and Mr. Buchanan, the principle of non-intervention was triumphantly maintained. The departure from that, and the attempt to engraft the doctrine of Congressional Intervention, in favor of slavery in the Territories, were fatal to our cause and gave the battle to the Republicans. I say this much, as a frank and honest expression of my opinion, without intending to attach blame to anybody; without intending to question the patriotism of anybody; without even intending to express an opinion, as to who was right and who was wrong. That one side or the other was wrong is self-evident; for both could not be right. We are therefore indebted to an error in [of] our own, for our signal defeat—it elected Lincoln. Hence, as we are not entirely blameless, it behooves us to temper our exasperation by calm reflection and prudent counsels. Hasty action is always unwise: it is superlative folly, when prompted by passion for which, our own indiscretion has created the existing occasion.

But "let the dead bury their dead." Let the conflict through which we have just passed, with all its acerbity and rancor be consigned to oblivion; and animated with a patriotic desire to rescue our country from impending dangers, let us take counsel with each other, as friends and fellow-citizens whose political interests and destiny are one.

I do not think the election of Lincoln a sufficient cause for secession. No man deprecates it more than I do. None is more implacably hostile to the avowed principles and policy of the Republican party. I trust I am second to no one, in an intelligent devotion to the rights and honor of the South. But he is legit-

3. The Democratic Party Convention of 1856, meeting in Cincinnati, reendorsed the principle of congressional nonintervention in respect to slavery in the national territories. The Dred Scott Decision of 1857 declared that congressional intervention to abolish slavery in the national territories was unconstitutional.

imately elected—elected in strict accordance with the Constitution, and therefore, being stricklers [sic] ourselves, for conformity on the part of others to the Constitution, let us practice our precept by observing it, on our part. If he obey[s] the Constitution, in his administration, we shall have suffered no injury by his election: if he violate[s] it, by aggressing upon our rights, we will resist it and the justice of that resistance will rally the united hearts and hands of all true patriots.

But it is contended by many, that we must anticipate aggression—assumed that it will come, and secede from the Union immediately to avoid it. I do not approve of such a course. But anticipating that it may come, prudence suggests that we begin, at once, to prepare to resist it.

I believe however, that, under the existing circumstances, it cannot come. The President is powerless, without the concurrence of both houses of Congress. But both are known to be opposed to the federal principles and policy of the Republican party. How is it possible then for Lincoln to commit any aggression upon the South? He cannot organize his administration except by the approval of the Senate; no measure can be adopted, without the action of Congress. He can do nothing of himself. He is at the mercy of Congress—subject really to its dictation—as powerless as Sampson shorn of his locks. Therefore, when it is asked, will you submit to the rule of Lincoln? I reply no; I am not under his *rule,* but under the rule of the government whose legislative department is known to be friendly to the constitutional rights of the South. *He* is the one who is under *rule*—bound hand and foot. I bid him defiance, while thus bound; but if the complexion of Congress shall change to that of hostility to my section, knock off his fetters and violate our rights, I will defy them all: and if I cannot obtain redress in the Union, then, trusting to the reserved sovereignty of the State, I will strike for separate independence out of the Union.

But the South has grievances of which to complain, far

more galling than the bare election of a Republican to the Presidency. The surrender of fugitive slaves is a constitutional obligation upon every State in the Union. Without such a guaranty the Union would never have been formed. It cannot long survive its continued and persistent disregard by the non-slaveholding States. The violation of it, by some, commenced almost simultaneously with the abolition agitation. It has "grown with its growth and strengthened with its strength," [and] now, in defiance of federal enactments, a majority of those States have passed stringent laws to obstruct and hinder the recovery of fugitive slaves. True, the cotton States have not suffered very considerably, on this score; that evil necessarily falls mainly upon the border States. But all the slave-holding States have felt and do now keenly feel this infidelity of their Northern sisters to their plain constitutional obligation. They have said but little however; they have submitted to it, almost without complaint. Amidst the almost unmixed evil, which I apprehend from the election of Lincoln, I see one good result, and that is, the awakening of the South to these great grievances. They ought not to be permanently submitted to; but promptly redressed, upon the united demand of the South. Let the appeal be made to the delinquent States.

Having presented these general views, I will venture a few suggestions as to the best course to be pursued. In justice to myself I must refer briefly to my position in 1850, when we were somewhat similarly excited. It is well known that I opposed the compromise measures, and acted with the Southern rights party. I did then as I would do now, under similar circumstances, and I am not conscious of any material change in the views which I entertained, touching the great questions involved in that contest. I was denounced then as a disunionist; and because I am not a disunionist now, I am charged with inconsistency and the abandonment of my Southern rights principles.—From all that has been said recently, the country doubtless believe, that I was an active participant in the contest of 1850—in its fiery debates and the extreme views entertained by many of the leaders of the Southern rights party. The truth is, I did not make a single speech during the contest, excepting a few remarks, not occupying ten minutes, in a meeting in Baldwin country, in which I then resided. I was on the bench of the Ocmulgee Circuit. I wrote but one letter, after the opening of the canvass for delegates, to the Convention, and that was after the election. I appeal to that for the evidence that I was not for secession then, and that I stood then, in reference to the action of the State, precisely where this communication will show that I stand now.

The letter alluded to, was written on the 5th of Nov., 1850, in reply to James S. Hook and others of Washington county, who asked my "opinion with reference to the policy to be pursued by our State," in the then emergency. After briefly reviewing the compromise measure, I said:

"What then is the proper line of policy for Georgia in the present emergency?

"The wrongs of which we complain are not peculiar to Georgia, but common to all the slaveholding States. Hence, in any action which our State may adopt, she should regard herself only as an integral part of the South and should act only in reference to the concurrence and cooperation of the slaveholding States. The interests of slavery and those of cotton, rice and sugar are identical, and must share the same fate, and therefore, at least the States engaged in these products[4] should be united in measures of redress or future security. Hence, I have never favored the policy of separate State secession—not that I question the right, but because I do not regard it an effectuel [sic] remedy for past wrongs or a potent safeguard against future aggressions.

---

4. Johnson meant the Lower South states: South Carolina, Georgia, Florida, Alabama, Mississippi, Louisiana, and Texas.

"Indeed, I am frank to say, that I would not dissolve this Union, by secession or otherwise, for what has already been done, if any assurance can be obtained from the North, that they will cease their aggressions and permit us to remain quietly in the Union. Our line of policy then, in my poor judgment, is to adopt such measures as will prevent all future encroachments upon our rights.—To render these effectual, they must meet the approval and co-operation of those States which grow cotton, rice and sugar."

These are my opinions now, so far as they are applicable to the existing circumstances. I am opposed to dissolution now, by secession or otherwise, and for reasons similar to those which controlled my opinion then.

The course which I then suggested for the State convention was contained in the following propositions:

2.[5] I would have our convention record the unanimous and strong protest of Georgia against the late acts of Congress, in reference to our Mexican territories and her unalterable determination never to yield another inch of ground to Northern encroachments."

3. Let the convention demand of Congress the repeal of the Mexican laws in Utah and New Mexico, against slavery,[6] so as to open the door of safe emigration thither, by the slaveholders of the South."

"4. The convention should demand of the Northern States, as a matter of loyalty to the Constitution, the repeal of those

5. Johnson started with Plank 2 because his Plank 1 had been only a declaration that the legislature must summon a convention of the people, to consider the proper remedy.

6. Johnson assumed, as did many congressmen, that in territories purchased from Mexico, Mexican law remained in force unless the United States Congress repealed or replaced it. A Mexican law had abolished slavery in these territories. The Compromise of 1850 had not replaced or repealed this abolition edict. Hence slavery had arguably been banned in these territories even though—indeed precisely because—Congress had avoided the subject.

legislative acts obstructing the recapture of fugitive slaves, to the end that the recent statute of Congress may be executed in good faith and without molestation under the forms of law."

"5. The convention should demand of the Northern States that they should suppress the abolition agitation, on the ground that it endangers the public peace and puts in jeopardy the friendly relations between these States.

"6. The convention should demand, in behalf of the South, perpetual exemption from future aggression."

"7. The Convention should require our State Legislature to adopt such measures of legislation as are necessary to place the State in a condition of the most ample preparation to meet all consequences which a continued disregard of our rights by the North may force upon us.

"Let these propositions be distinctly propounded to the North for their solemn reflection and to our sister Southern States for their co-operation and adoption. And let us invite the latter to send delegates to a Southern Congress to meet in Milledgeville on the 4th of July, 1851—*not to dissolve the Union, but to devise measures for their enforcement, with the view to preserve the rights of the South in the Union.*"

These were my opinions as to the proper course for Georgia to adopt in 1850. As far as they are applicable to the present crisis, I would advise their adoption now. Then I would say:

1. Let this Legislature call a convention of the people, at such time as may be deemed most convenient, to consider and determine what the State should do; and also, in the meantime, put the State in a condition to meet any emergency.

2. Let that Convention reaffirm the "Georgia Platform" of 1850[7] and demand the repeal of all laws passed by any of the

7. For a description of the critical Georgia Platform of 1850, see Chapter 3, note 11, p. 69. Note that Johnson, like Stephens and Hill, wished to expand the pledge of "resistance" to include not only *congressional* but also *northern* nullification of the Fugitive Slave Law. All three Unionists thus underlined

non-slaveholding States, which obstruct the execution, in good faith, of the act of Congress for the rendition of fugitive slaves.

3. Let that Convention appeal to the Northern States to suppress by all legitimate measures the slavery agitation, as subversive of the peace and fraternity between the States of this Union.

4. Let that Convention ask a consultation with the other Southern States, either in a Congress for that purpose, or in such other manner as may be best calculated to secure concert of action.

I repeat what I said in the letter alluded to.

"As to the means a Southern Congress ought to adopt to enforce these propositions, it would be presumption in me to venture a suggestion. I prefer rather to stand mute before the wisdom of its counsels and bow submissively to its decisions. I am willing to confide the interest, the honor and rights of the South in the hands of such a body; and sure I feel, that its moral influence, representing as it would, the patriotism, the intelligence and firm resolve of the South, would be potent to save the Union and awaken the Northern States to the danger with which their misguided fanaticism has imperiled it."

I should hope that a firm and earnest appeal by the South to the Northern States would be heeded; that they would, under a sense of Constitutional obligation, repeal their "personal liberty bills," and cease to hinder the surrender of fugitive slaves.—I repeat, a continued and persistent disregard of our rights, in this particular, by the non-slaveholding States, cannot and ought not to be submitted to. It is time for the South to demand exemption from the agitation of slavery, from unjustifiable interference with our domestic peace and security, from further aggressions upon our rights and the faithful ob-

---

their endorsement of "resistance," even while they denied that secession, the "last resort," was yet the necessary form of "resistance."

servance by the Northern States of the requirements and guarantees of the Constitution. Let the business of redress be begun now and prosecuted to a final consummation. Let every effort be made and every means be exhausted to restore the Union back to what it was intended to be, by its founders. If we fail in this, which I will not anticipate, then the interest, rights, peace and honor of the South will require a dissolution of the Union.

Thanking you gentlemen for the complimentary terms of your note, I am

Truly and faithfully, your ob't serv't,

HERSCHEL V. JOHNSON

6

Henry L. Benning's Secessionist Speech,
Monday Evening, November 19

*Secessionists' first choice to turn back the Unionists' offen-
sive would have been Howell Cobb. But with Cobb lingering in
Washington, a secessionist in Georgia had to be substituted. An
instant oration had to be produced, which could be presented
the night before the legislature passed the convention bill,
thereby ending the Milledgeville evening debate. Henry L. Benning eagerly accepted the assignment, especially as a substitute
for Howell Cobb.*

*Benning, the least famous and most intellectual of these
seven protagonists, had long resented Howell Cobb. The resentment went back to their shared years at the University of
Georgia. As a student, Henry Benning had outperformed Howell
Cobb. Benning thought that the brightest patriarch should go
the farthest. Instead Cobb, the better politician, became a long-
term governmental titan while Benning, the better abstraction-
ist, became a one term Associate Justice of the Georgia Supreme
Court.*

Benning issued his most important judicial opinion in Pa-

dleford vs Savannah *(1854)*. *The jurist insisted that no United States Supreme Court decision need bind a state court. State and federal courts, argued Benning, were "coordinate and co-equal." That extreme states' rights position sustained Benning, a large slaveholder, throughout his futile chase after Howell Cobb, first as an unimportant delegate to the Nashville Southern Convention of 1850, then as a failed congressional States' Rights candidate in 1851, then as chairman of the Georgia delegation that walked out of the Democratic National Convention in 1860.*

Henry Benning's secessionist oration of November 19, 1860 displayed his best qualities: sharp abstractions, judicial logic, and states' rights zealotry. The speech would catapult Benning forward, as sometimes chairman of the Georgia Secession Convention and as Georgia's Commissioner to the Virginia Convention, where he would repeat his Milledgeville oratorical success. But then, old slights would recur. Howell Cobb would become a power in the Confederate government and Benning a second-rank Confederate general. Still, Henry Benning's wartime nickname, "Old Rock," fit his image when he rose to the occasion in Milledgeville. He was the old states' righter, standing like a rock against "Black Republicans," whom he found even more infuriating than Howell Cobb.[1]

Fellow Citizens: The points for our consideration are, what is the disease—the precise disease under which the South is

---

1. Posterity lacks a full-scale biography of the intriguing Benning but a superb biographical essay fortunately exists: James C. Cobb, "The Making of a Secessionist: Henry L. Benning and the Coming of the Civil War," *Georgia Historical Quarterly,* 60 (1976):313–23. We have transcribed Benning's speech from Henry L. Benning, *Speech on Federal Relations... Delivered in the Hall of the House of Representatives, Nov. 6th, 1860* (n.p., n.d.). A copy of the pamphlet is in the University of Georgia Library. Note that Benning's oration is misdated on the title page; see the discussion above, Introduction, note 24.

laboring, and what is the remedy? I propose to endeavor to maintain several propositions showing, I think, what that disease is, and also what the remedy is for that disease. In doing this, I beg to assure you beforehand that my wishes are to convince your judgments, not to inflame your passions. Without further preface, I will proceed to consider those propositions.

My first proposition is that the election of Mr. Lincoln to the Presidency of the United States means the abolition of slavery, as soon as the party which elected him shall acquire the power to do the deed. The truth of that proposition is to be deduced from all the acts of that party in the past. It is literally true that that party has in the past manifested its hostility to slavery in exact proportion to its capacity to do it. When it consisted of individual members, it contented itself with individual opposition to the execution of the Fugitive Slave Law in the free States, and with the persecution of the master pursuing his fugitive thither; acquiring more strength, and getting into Congress, it began with the presentation of abolition petitions to induce Congress to take jurisdiction over the subject.[2] In the last few years it has obtained possession of many of the Northern States, and whenever it has done so, it has enacted laws nullifying the Constitution in the fugitive slave clause. This is the past. Its last great act is the election of Mr. Lincoln as President of the United States,— Mr. Lincoln, who has declared eternal hostility to slavery. That is the sum of his creed, that creed on which he was elected—eternal hostility to slavery. He has been put upon us by the Black Republicans, notwithstanding remonstrance

2. Benning here referred to the beginning of the Gag Rule Controversy, in the Fall of 1835, when antislavery groups first massively petitioned Congress to abolish slavery in Washington, D.C., and elsewhere. Congress gagged such petitions by refusing to allow them to be discussed, a procedure which lasted until December, 1844.

and entreaty—appeals to their patriotism, appeals to their
affection, appeals to their fear. Now I say this great act of
theirs not only ratifies and reaffirms all of the bad past, but
it foretells the future. It signifies to you that in the future,
as in the past, this party will, to the utmost of its ability,
harm slavery. And this is not surprising. It is in accordance
with a law of nature,—with the law that cause will produce
its effect. This party *hates* slavery; that is the word—hates
slavery. The chosen leaders, Mr. Lincoln and Mr. Seward,
proclaim that there is an irrepressible, eternal conflict between the slave States and the free. Another chosen leader,
Mr. Sumner, calls the sentiment a "sacred animosity," that
is, religion. Now this party, actuated by this depth of hate
towards slavery, would be untrue to its past history, if it did
not exert all its power to destroy slavery. The only question,
therefore, is as to when the party shall acquire the ability
to destroy it. I say then, that the meaning of Mr. Lincoln's
election to the Presidency is the abolition of slavery as soon
as the Republican party shall have acquired the strength to
abolish it.

My second proposition is that the North will soon acquire
that power, unless something is done to prevent it. I dare say
every one present will agree that this is almost a self-evident
proposition. The North has now eighteen States, and the South
fifteen. The whole of the public territory of the United States
may at this time be said to be Northern territory. This is pain-
fully true, and it is conclusive evidence that we shall have no
more slave States from the public territory. This territory has
an area sufficient to form twenty States of 50,000 square miles
each. Add to these the other eighteen, and you have thirty-
eight. But this is not all. Some of the slave States are in the
process of becoming free States. The last census shows that
Delaware has decreased in its number of slaves. Probably the
same is true of Maryland and Kentucky, whilst Virginia and
Missouri have barely held their own. In process of time, and

that no long time, these States will become free States. North Carolina and Tennessee will soon follow them. Then slavery will be compressed into the eight[3] cotton States.

Gentlemen, I pray you to realize this as a great fact, that there are causes already in operation, which, if allowed to continue in operation, will drive down all the slaves into the cotton States, and you know they are but eight. When that time comes, and indeed long before that time comes, the North—the Black Republican party (for that will be the North) will have it in its power only to amend the Constitution, and take what power it pleases upon the subject of slavery. It will then take the power to emancipate your slaves, and to hang you if you resist their emancipation.

But we have reason to believe from what this party has already done, that it will not wait until it can acquire this great majority of the States, and thus amend the Constitution. As soon as it can acquire the physical power to act, it will act, and will abolish slavery. The Constitution, with that party, is already a dead letter—a thing void, under the operation of the "higher law."[4] The only question, therefore, will be one of physical power. And that power they are rapidly acquiring, and will soon acquire, unless something is done to prevent it. And this is my second proposition.

My third is that abolition would be to the South one of the direst evils of which the mind can conceive. Let us look at it for a moment. When abolition comes by the decree of the North, it will come at a time when the South is so weak that the North will feel that she will be perfectly able to accomplish the deed.

3. Benning here added Arkansas to the usual list of seven Lower South states: South Carolina, Georgia, Florida, Alabama, Mississippi, Louisiana, and Texas.

4. A famous phrase of New York's United States Senator William H. Seward, used in Congress in 1850. Seward, soon to be a leading Republican, here implied that moral law must take precedence over constitutional law, if antislavery action was indeed unconstitutional.

Still the South will not be so weak that she will feel herself
utterly powerless. The cotton States will, at that time, have a
large population of slaves, perhaps a larger population of slaves
than of whites; but the population of the whites will be respectable. The decree will excite an intense hatred between the
whites on one side, and the slaves and the North on the other.
Very soon a war between the whites and the blacks will spon-
taneously break out everywhere. It will be in every town, in
every village, in every neighborhood, in every road. It will be
a war of man with man—a war of extermination. Quickly the
North will intervene, and of course take sides with the party
friendly towards them—the blacks. The coalition will exter-
minate the white race, or expel them from the land, to wander
as vagabonds over the face of the earth. That will be the fate
of the cotton States, so far as the men are concerned; and as
for the women, they will call upon the mountains to fall upon
them. That will be the end of the white race that now exists
in the cotton States, and the black race will take possession of
our goodly land, and convert it into another Jamaica, or St.
Domingo. But that is not all. Our Northern friends will begin
to covet the good lands thus held by the blacks, as they do all
good lands within their reach, and they will gradually encroach
upon them and drive off the negroes. Under this process, more
and more energetically pursued, the negroes will follow the
fate of their late masters, and be exterminated, and the Yankee
will tread your soil as lord. Am I not right then in saying that
abolition is one of the direst evils that the mind can imagine?

Thus then we have data from which we may announce this
position: that abolition, dire evil as it is, is inevitable, unless
something is done either to mollify this hostility to slavery on
the part of the North, or to prevent the North from acquiring
the power to abolish slavery. Whatever remedy is proposed,
must be tried by these two characteristics. Having either, it
will be sufficient; having neither, it will be wholly insufficient.

I beg you to observe another thing. Some have thought that a remedy to our evils would be to have the fugitive slave law enforced on the part of the non-slaveholding States. True, we need that; for at the North that law is a dead letter. We need, therefore, a remedy for that evil; but that question bears no higher relation to that great one, the intention to abolish slavery, than a cent does to a dollar. It is a mere trifle compared with the question whether or not slavery shall be abolished at the South. Is not that so? Our remedy must be a remedy for this prospective abolition. Any remedy for that will almost certainly be a remedy for the other, and the remedy for that is what we are now to seek for.

Then, as I said, any remedy that will be sufficient to prevent the abolition of slavery, must have one of the two characteristics which have been mentioned; either a capacity to change the will of the North, and make them willing to let slavery exist as it is, or else the capacity to prevent the North from acquiring the power to abolish it. If it fails in either of these respects, it is no remedy: it does not reach the disease.

What now are the remedies suggested or supposable to prevent the North from abolishing slavery? First, I will consider those in the Union, and I will suppose as strong a case as I can. Suppose a convention, regularly called of all the States of the Union, suppose that Convention should so amend the Constitution of the United States, as to make it say that all the public territory should be equally, or in proper proportion, divided between the North and the South, and say further that it should be the duty of the General Government, and even of the non-slaveholding States, to protect slavery. Suppose we could get such an amendment as this to the Constitution.

Still, even this would be no remedy, and the reason is, you cannot depend upon the North for any guaranty she gives you. She may stipulate and promise, and make Constitutions, but so far as slavery is concerned, she will observe none of these.

She holds slavery to be a sin and a crime, "a league with hell and covenant with death";[5] and holding this sentiment, she does not consider herself bound to keep any covenant or agreement favorable to slavery, and the only question with her as to any such agreement or covenant, is as to whether she has the strength to violate it with impunity. Do you not know that this is true of the Black Republican party, which has now become the North? And holding as the North does these doctrines, you cannot fasten her by any compact, league or covenant which you may make with her. Constitutions are of no efficacy, promises are of no avail, because she holds them to be void when they favor slavery. Even, then, if we could get such amendments as these to the Constitution, the remedy would be ineffective, insufficient. Why? because the North would not keep them, and that same hatred to slavery would still exist. It is ineradicable; not only so, but that same process of acquiring the power to abolish slavery would go on, though not quite so fast. New free States would still be coming into the Union, and old States would be transforming themselves into free States. And the new slave States admitted into the Union from below the new dividing line, would not remain slave States long. Lying on the same parallels as the border slave States, they would be subject to the same causes which are now operating on the border slave States and transforming them into free States. All the slaves would gradually sink down into Texas and Arkansas, and finally even these new States would become free States merely by the process of declaring themselves such. So that this measure, notwithstanding it seems so promising, is no remedy to the disease. It does not meet the case. It only puts off the evil day a little while, to make it a darker day when it does come; for come it will.

It seems then that even amendments of the Constitution

5. A famous statement by Massachusetts' William Lloyd Garrison of Massachusetts, the leading abolitionist and editor of *The Liberator*.

so great as these would be no remedy. They would lack both of the essential characteristics of the remedy. They would not suffice to change the North's hostility to slavery, nor to prevent the North from acquiring the power to abolish slavery.

This is a case which we have merely supposed. Nobody dreams that a general convention of the States would concede us such amendments as those supposed. Nobody at the South who merely goes for a convention, raises his voice so high as to demand such amendments. No; but what do gentlemen of the South propose as remedies? I now come to consider these.

And first, as to Mr. Stephens. Mr. Stephens, as I understand him, proposes that there shall be a convention of the Southern States; that this convention shall remonstrate with the Northern States which have violated the Constitution in refusing to execute the Fugitive Slave Law, and shall demand of them the repeal of their obnoxious laws, and shall plainly declare to them that if they do not repeal those laws, the South will dissolve the Union. This, if I understand it, is his whole remedy. Now I say, men of Georgia, that this remedy does not look at the great disease—it does not touch it. It has reference merely to the Fugitive Slave Law, a matter which I think is comparatively a trifle in this great controversy. This would be a sufficient objection to the plan of Mr. Stephens. If it be true that the case which I have supposed would be no remedy, much more must it be true that this can be none, for this falls short of that by a thousand leagues.

I proceed, however, to discuss it a little further. And the first remark which I make on it is, that small as it is, it is unattainable. I say that it would be a vain thing to call the Southern States together and induce them to make this remonstrance to the non-slaveholding States, with the announcement that if the remonstrance was not heeded they would go out of the Union. The North, the Black Republican party, would disregard any such remonstrance. It would laugh in our faces. In order to get that demand conceded, it would be necessary to overthrow the Black Republican party at the North—it would be necessary to have a party get into power there friendly to slavery. Therefore, I say it would be necessary to overthrow the Black Republican party.

Now I say it would be a hopeless undertaking to overthrow the Black Republican party. That party now has at the North the press, the pulpit, the schoolmaster, the schoolmistress, the governors, the legislatures, the judges, the county officers, the town officers—all official life; it has on its side the antipathy to slavery, which is almost universal at the North, and now it takes possession of the general government and all its power and patronage. Every man at the North who has office, from the governor down to the constable, holds it by the tenure of his hatred to slavery. Can you overthrow a party thus deeply rooted by a remonstrance and by a threat? Why, we have told them all through this campaign that if they elected Lincoln to the Presidency this Union would be dissolved. And they have received the threat with mockery and scorn. You could no more dislodge this party from its seat at the North by remonstrance and menace, than you could expel the English from Gibralter by the blast of a ram's horn. (Applause.)

I say, then, that the first objection I have to this plan, even so far as the Fugitive Slave Law is concerned, is that it is unattainable. Another objection is that it involves delay, and a great deal of delay. First you have to call a convention of individual Southern States. The Legislatures of those States will first have to assemble. Each of these things will take up time. After that, remonstrance has to be sent to each individual State that passed the obnoxious laws, and each has to consider whether it will repeal them or not. This will take up additional time; and in the interval Mr. Lincoln, with all the power which he, as President of the United States, can exert, will set about preparing to defeat your purpose of going out of the Union in case your remonstrance shall be disregarded by the culprit States.

And what will he be able to do? There is, you say, a majority of the Senate and House of Representatives in the present Congress opposed to his policy. Grant it; still he can do a great deal to harm you. You have now much the largest proportion of arms and ammunition in your arsenals. The President has the power to order these to be sent away from you. That would be an immense loss to you. And then there is in the non-slaveholding States an organization vast in its numbers, ready at a word to assume a military form, trained already in soldierly exercises. Are you willing that Mr. Lincoln shall have the opportunity of taking your arms from your arsenals, and putting them into the hands of the Wide Awakes? Mr. Stephens' plan would give him that opportunity.

Another objection I have to that plan is, that it would not be a remedy for even the small disease which it proposes to remedy, the violation of the Fugitive Slave Law by the Northern States. Suppose the obnoxious laws of these States were repealed, would that relieve the South? Why, these laws have never, I believe, been enforced against a single Southern man, notwithstanding some of them have been in existence for years, and many cases of escape have occurred. No, the trouble is that the hostility of the *people* of the North to slavery is so great that the public authorities of the United States can not execute the laws of the General Government; and as long as that hostility remains, the same difficulty will remain in executing it. When a people is universally against a law, you can not execute it; and so I say it would be a vain thing to expect the least aid to the recovery of fugitive slaves from the repeal of those obnoxious laws—a perfectly vain thing.

I think, then, this remedy proposed by Mr. Stephens is wholly inadequate. What is the remedy of Mr. Hill? I am not sure that I understand him as to his remedy. His plan is this, if I understand it: that there should be a convention of the people of Georgia, or perhaps of the Southern States, and a

demand on the President to enforce the Fugitive Slave Law;
and in the event the North resisted its enforcement, to call out
the military force of the South to compel the North to observe
the law.

Gentlemen, this plan seems to me to labor under all the
objections to that of Mr. Stephens; but there are others peculiar
to it. It certainly involves delay, as much or more than than
[sic] the other; because before an opportunity shall occur when
the North shall resist the action of the Federal Government in
the execution of the Fugitive Slave Law, four or more years
may elapse. The Southern people are afraid to go into the
Northern States for their slaves. A case to set this plan in
motion may not occur for years—may never occur.

But there is an additional objection peculiar to this plan.
It calls upon the *President* to enforce the Fugitive Slave Law.
Why, the President has always done his duty in enforcing that
law. That is not the difficulty. It is not any number of regular
soldiers, or Southern soldiers that you need to execute the law;
it is a *posse comitatus* of citizens in the Northern States themselves that you need. And this you cannot have as long as
hostility there to slavery is as great as it is. Public opinion
rises up in vast mobs against your attempt to carry back your
slave.

The idea of the President's calling out the whole military
force of the South has a show of grandeur about it, but it is all
show.

Another remedy or plan sometimes spoken of, is to fight
in the Union. I say no, for if we do, we fight to great disad-
vantage. The Constitution declares that no State shall make
a compact with another State; shall make a treaty with a foreign nation; shall levy any tax on imports, or on exports, or on
tonnage; shall coin money, emit bills of credit, or make anything but gold and silver coin a tender in the payment of debts.
The Constitution gives the war power to the General Govern-

ment. Now, when the States go to fight in the Union, it is of course to be assumed that they shall do so constitutionally. If they fight there constitutionally, they will fight shorn of half their strength, and fight as isolated units. On the other hand, the General Government will have all of its power, and all of its prestige. It will also have the benefit of the question whether the citizens of the fighting States do not owe their allegiance to it rather than to those States. It is plain that it will be bad, fighting the General Government in the Union. This plan, too, involves delay. When is the war to commence, if you wait to fight in the Union? Will you wait until the North has it in her power to abolish slavery? If you wait till then, resistance will be vain. I think, however, that this plan has not been seriously entertained by many reflecting persons as the one the South ought to adopt.

These three are all the plans for obtaining our rights in the Union that I have heard spoken of. The difficulty with them all is that they do not reach that great disease for which they are prescribed; they do not operate on that *will* of the North, which is fixed to destroy slavery. They do not operate on that process by which the North is fast acquiring the *power* to destroy slavery. What then? It follows that there is not within the Union any remedy by which we can escape abolition, and therefore if we wish for a remedy, a remedy we must seek for outside of the Union. [Bursts of applause.] I say, gentlemen, that follows as a necessary conclusion if these propositions are true, and of their truth you are to judge.

Well, I say that a separation from the North would be a complete remedy for the disease—a complete remedy for both diseases, a remedy not merely to prevent abolition, but also to heal the fugitive slave ulcer.

How would it do this? If you were to separate from the North, the *power* to abolish slavery by the North would be taken away. That is clear. The *will* to do so would also cease.

Slavery exists in Cuba, exists in Brazil, and the North has much commerce with both, yet we never hear of its stealing a slave from either. Let us examine this a little further.—What is it that gives abolitionism at the North such power? It is this: Abolitionism enters into their politics—all the offices of the State are at length held by the tenure of hatred to slavery. "Political capital" is made of it. No party in Canada, or England, or France, does or can make any political capital out of the slavery of the South. And so it would soon be at the North, if the South was a separate people.

I say, then, that whenever the South is separated from the North, the question of slavery will go out of the politics of the North, and in its stead other questions will spring up which will occupy all their time and attention: such questions for example, as the tariff, the disposition of the public lands, internal improvements, and various others. And there would then be parties amongst themselves on these questions. The Western States are an agricultural people, the Eastern and middle a manufacturing and commercial people. The two latter would desire heavy protective duties, the former would resist such duties. Amidst the distractions and the quarrels that would ensue on this and other subjects, there would be but little time to give to fugitive slaves, or to the slave question. I believe that so far from harboring those slaves, they would expel them if they came over into their borders. Already some of the Western States have laws expelling free negroes—it is only when receiving a negro as an injury to some master, that they will receive a negro. The feeling from which this conduct springs would soon pass away, after a separation. Interest would take the place of prejudice, then become abstract. They would leave us our slaves to help to make the cotton they would want, as England does. So we see that we have a perfect remedy for both diseases, in immediate secession. (Plaudits.)

That is not all: If we were separate from the North, we

could put an end to the alarming process by which the slave population is draining off into the cotton States. The mere act of separation would have that tendency. *Fear*—the fear that slaves will escape to the North by the under-ground railroad, and otherwise, is the chief cause of the drain. After a separation, stock in the under-ground rail-road would cease to pay, and the road would suspend business. What might be lacking, we could easily obtain by making suitable laws, such as a law laying a tax on every slave coming from above a certain parallel of latitude. You could enact any law of this kind, as the States would be all of one feeling on the subject, and it would be to the interest of all of them that slavery should be diffused over the whole extent of their territory. But even at the worst, the border States, if they should become free States, would not be strong enough to harm the cotton States. The cotton States have almost six hundred thousand square miles of territory, the border States less than three hundred thousand. With this relative proportion of territory, it would be impossible for the border States to interfere with slavery in the cotton States, and therefore even though the border States should become hostile to slavery, a case hardly supposable, it would not be in their power to harm us.

The separation from the North would then be a perfect remedy for *all* diseases. If that is so we certainly ought to adopt it, unless the objections to it are too great; unless the evils which it would entail are greater than those that would come from abolition, and greater than those that come from the nullification of the fugitive slave clause of the constitution.

What are the objections to a separation from the North? Let us consider them calmly. The first is, that not enough of the slave States will separate to make it effectual. I deny this. I say that if one or two of the cotton States go out, all the cotton States will go out, and that if all the cotton States go out, all the border States will soon follow. State will rush to the side of State, as a brother rushes to the side of a brother when about

to be overborne by a mortal adversary, though it may be that
he himself would not have begun the fight. This mere feeling
of fraternity would be enough, but it will have the aid of interest. In a separate government with us, the border States
would have for their manufactures that monopoly of our rich
markets which the North now has—whereas, in a separate
government with the North they would have to encounter in
all markets, a profitless competition with the North.

And then upon these great questions they are agreed with
us; that is to say, they are agreed to the extent that they do
not consider slavery an evil, and that they feel an interest in
maintaining it, whilst they are not agreed with the north. I
have no fear that if the cotton States should go out of the Union,
the other Southern States would fail to follow; but if they did
[not follow], I say boldly that we should be able ourselves to
maintain our cause.—(Loud cheers.) If they choose to keep their
connection with the northern states let them do so. Men of
Georgia! it is our business to save ourselves. (Continued applause.) And if nothing else will save us but going out of the
Union, we must go out of the Union, however much we may
deplore it.

I merely wish now to say, that if these States do not come
at first, they will come at last. They will *come,* and we may act
upon the assumption that they will come.

What is the next objection to a separation? "We are not
prepared to resist, the North would crush us." I say in answer
to that objection, that in the first place, we are as well prepared
as the North—better prepared than the North. From the best
information I can obtain, there is now a larger proportion of
the public arms and munitions at the South than at the North.
Then we have a larger fund of military knowledge at the South.
I believe there is not a single State Military school at the North.
But we have one in Virginia, said to be almost equal to that
at West Point; one or two in South Carolina that turn out
accomplished soldiers, one in Georgia, one in Kentucky, one in
Tennessee, one in Alabama; all of which are schools of a high

order. These schools will furnish our army with most accomplished officers, and when you have good officers, you will soon have good men.

We have more financial power and resources than the North has. We have an article which England must have. I might almost say the same of France. To deprive England of cotton would be the same as to deprive 4,000,000 of her subjects of the means of subsistence, and to throw them out to work anarchy and revolution. This she would never consent to. Thus our cotton would be an unfailing supply of money to us.

The temptation of England would be great to take sides against her rival the North, the only people that successfully competes with her in her ocean dominion. She never hesitates when her interests are at stake, and she would have a ready pretence in the San Juan and the Central America questions.

She has ships enough to destroy the entire navy which the North would have, and to enter the harbor of New York and Boston, and with the improved artillery of the day destroy these cities in a few hours.

On the other hand the North cut off from Southern cotton, rice, tobacco, and other Southern products would lose three fourths of her commerce, and a very large proportion of her manufactures. And thus those great fountains of finance would sink very low.

I say then that we would have ample power to maintain our independence in spite of the North.

Again, suppose the South does wait to prepare? Whilst she is preparing the North will also be preparing, and being in possession of the general government she will prepare twice as fast, and twice as well. Mr. Seward has already proclaimed (in his late speech at Lansing)[6] that one single Republican administration will be sufficient to do the business for slavery.

But indeed there will be no war. The effect at the North

6. Benning here referred to William H. Seward's speech in Lansing, Michigan, in early September, 1860. No good text apparently survives.

of our separation would be a commercial crisis, a bankruptcy
greater than has ever prevailed there before. The very separation itself would produce the effect. Would the North in such
a condition as that declare war against the South? Property in
the North, and particularly in its vast emporiums of commerce
would sink to a mere nominal value: nobody would be able to
pay the necessary taxes for the war. There would be nothing
in the Treasury, and no ability to borrow. Her soldiers would
have to be shipped at a vast expense (for the border States
would not suffer them to go through their borders) to the cotton
States, perhaps around the dangerous coast of Florida, and be
sent as far as to Galveston. Every soldier would cost according
to an estimate which I have seen $1000 per year. They could
not raise an army. A few persons might volunteer for the sake
of bread, none would for any other reason. Under these circumstances could they expect to conquer even us of the cotton
States, although they might number 18,000,000 of people, and
we only 5,000,000?

Why, look at Prussia. For seven long years she resisted
the combined power of France, Austria and Russia. It happened
that she had taken Silasia [sic], and they wished to deprive
her of it, but she, with her 6,000,000 or 7,000,000 of people
successfully resisted their 60,000,000 or 70,000,000 and held
Silasia [sic].[7] The Prussians were fighting upon their own soil,
as we would be upon ours; and we would fight there in such a
cause as ours would be, not only like them but even with the
spirit of Leonidas when he [defended] Thermopylae.[8] Applause.

Then our very climate is a terror to men of northern cli-

7. In the Third Silesian, or Seven Years War, 1756–63, Prussia made
good her claim to Silesia, which was part of Poland, despite the numerically
superior combined armies of France, Austria, and Russia.

8. Leonidas I, King of Sparta, who, with the 300 survivors of his original
army of 4,000 fought to the death against the invading Persians at the mountain pass of Thermopylae in 480 B. C. Leonidas and his men were annihilated,
whereupon the Persians destroyed Athens.

mate. They think that yellow fever and other forms of fever almost as bad fill up all of our summers and our autumns, the time of campaigns. Who would volunteer for the glory of dying of black vomit? It is true, I believe, that in the revolutionary war not a single northern soldier could be produced for love or money to come south of York Town.

And after all, suppose they should conquer us, would that bring back to them the 4,000,000 bales of our cotton, the handling of which they so much covet? Certainly not. Now, however richly endowed the people of the North may be with the quality of courage, they are more richly endowed with the faculty of calculation. And they would well count the cost of the war before they entered on it. Already one of their principal organs, the Tribune,[9] has proclaimed that any State had the right to secede at will. They will not attempt to coerce us, but if they should, we shall be able to repel the attempt.

Another objection raised to separation is, that in such an event we should suffer a great loss in the public treasury, in the public lands and in the navy. Now, gentlemen, so far as the public lands are concerned, they will be worth nothing to us; we shall never get a foot of them. The party in power will, on account of the preponderance of northern emigration take possession of the whole of the public lands. They are in favor of giving the land to settlers, or selling it at a mere nominal value.

Our share in the public lands whether they be considered as a source of revenue or a source of political power is rather insignificant.

So far as the public treasury is concerned, we shall suffer but a small loss in parting with our share of it. It is constantly employing itself to meet the current demands of the govern-

9. Horace Greeley's *New York Tribune,* whose well-known proposed policy of "letting the erring [southern] brothers go in peace" had some less well-known qualifications.

ment, and it never has in, at any one time, more than a few
millions of dollars. Again, if the North takes the public treasury
they must take it with its burdens, with the public debt, and
this is so heavy that our share of it would be far greater than
our part of the money in the treasury.

And as for our loss of our share in the navy, it must be
remembered that the navy is small, and many of the ships out
of vogue and worthless for service. And consequently, if we
should fail to get a single ship, our loss would not be very great.
Yet, I shall be greatly disappointed if we shall not find every
gallant son of the South in command of a ship, coming with
all sail set into some southern harbor as soon as he hears the
news that the South has struck for independence.

Thus it will be seen that the losses would be small which
a separation would entail on the South. What would be the
gains? There are, by virtue of federal legislation and the working of the union, a number of drains, some of vast magnitude,
through which the money of the South is incessantly flowing
to the North. There is the vast drain occasioned by the tariff;
the drain occasioned by the navigation laws; the drain in slaves
occasioned by the under-ground railroad; the drain occasioned
by an excess of the public expenditures being made at the
North; the drain occasioned by the foreign goods consumed by
the South, coming through the North instead of coming directly; the drain occasioned by the money spent by southern
travelers at the North. A separation from the North would cut
off all these drains, and turn them back on the South to enrich
its manufactures, commerce and agriculture. This subject is so
important that it will require me to go somewhat into partic-
ulars. I will proceed to do so.

The average rate of duty imposed by the present tariff, is
nearly twenty per cent.[10] Every one knows that the effect of a

10. A duty on imported goods of 20 percent, thus raising the American

duty on foreign goods, is to raise the price, not only of those
goods, but also of corresponding domestic goods to the extent
of the duty. Therefore, the consumer, when he consumes domestic goods, pays as much duty to the home manufacturer as
he pays to the government when he consumes foreign goods.
If then we find out the amount of domestic goods consumed,
we can tell how much duty the consumers of the country pay
to the home manufacturers.

The question then is, what is the quantity of northern
manufactures consumed by the South?

What is the criterion by which we should measure the
relative quantities of consumption of the two sections? It is, I
think their ability to consume; that is, it is the amount of their
annual productions. This I regard as a better test than population. The latter, however, would be more favorable to the
South.

Taking the quantity of productions as the criterion, what
is the quantity of the productions of the North, and what the
quantity of those of the South[?] After a somewhat laborious
examination of the census returns of 1850, I have come to the
conclusion that the South's share of the productions for the
year, and the years since that was one-third, and the North's
two thirds. It would take up too much time to state the par-
ticulars by which I arrived at this conclusion. I beg leave, therefore, to assume that the South's share of the productions of the
country is one-third and the North's two thirds.

In 1850, according to that year's census the total manufactures of the Union, consumed at home, amounted to a little
over $1,000,000,000, of which the South's share was
$167,000,000, and the North's the rest. One-third of this
$1,000,000,000 is $333,000,000. This then was the part con-

---

price of those foreign goods the same 20 percent. This 20 percent rate, imposed
in the Tariff of 1857, was usually considered on the low side, but secessionists
such as Benning considered it still atrociously exploitative.

sumed by the South. Say that in this part was included the whole of her own manufactures, then the part of the North's manufactures consumed by her must have been $167,000,000.

Since 1850 manufactures have, according to the best information I can obtain, increased at the rate of at least seven per cent per year. And the prosperity of the South, during the same period, has been at least equal to that of the North.

Consequently the quantity of Northern Manufactures consumed by the South in [1860],[11] must have been about $284,000,000.

Let us grant that the price of a small part of these was not enhanced by the tariff—say of $34,000,000. Then the quantity, the price of which was enhanced by the tariff was $250,000,000. The rate at which the price was enhanced was, as we have seen, 20 per cent., consequently the amount of the drain from the South to the North, for 1860, was $50,000,000. Fifty millions of dollars was, therefore, the sum which the South in 1860 paid to the North without receiving one cent in return. It was a mere bounty to the North.

The "navigation laws" are acts of Congress which give to American vessels a monopoly of the coasting trade, a monopoly of the indirect trade, that is a monopoly of transporting the goods of a foreign nation, which do not come directly from it, but come through some other nation. The fishing bounty acts, and the light bounty acts may also perhaps be included under the head of "Navigation Laws." The former of these gives so much money in bounty to vessels engaged in cod fisheries, and the latter impose a duty of fifty cents a ton on all foreign vessels entering our harbors.

The effect of the monopoly of the coasting trade is to exclude American vessels from competition with the cheap car-

---

11. Benning's text reads 1850, which is a misleading typographical error.

rying vessels of England and Holland, and the rest of Europe; and consequently to enhance the price of the freight in the coasting trade. To the extent of this enhancement, the monopoly increases to the consumer, the price of the goods transported, coastwise, and confers a bounty on the shipowner. What is the extent of the enhancement?

The average freight on the goods going coastwise between the North and the South, I think we may safely estimate at six per cent. Now of this six per cent. I think it will be equally safe to set down two per cent. as due to the monopoly. The whole amount of Northern goods, consumed by the South, was as we have seen $284,000,000. Of these, I estimate that $200,000 came coastwise. Then the freight on them was $12,000,000, and the part of that freight due to the monopoly was $4,000,000.

Of these $4,000,000, a part was to the Northern ship owners, and a part to the Southern—to each in proportion to his tonage [sic]. The tonage in the coasting trade was nearly 2,500,000 tons, of which the North had nearly four-fifths, and the South a little over one-fifth, consequently, the part paid to Northern ship owners, as bounty under the coasting trade monopoly was $3,200,000. This was the coasting trade drain.

The indirect imports for the year ending the 30th of June, 1859, amounted to $36,915,570. Of these, about $35,000,000 were consumed in the country, and of course the consumers of them had to pay the enhancement of the freights on them, occasioned by the monopoly of transporting them enjoyed by American vessels. The whole freight on these goods, I estimate at 12 ½ per cent., of which at least 3 ½ per cent. was due, I think to the monopoly. This would make the sum paid by the consumers, on account of the monopoly $1,225,000. Of this sum, the Southern consumers paid one-third, say $408,000. The South had but one seventh of the foreign shipping—consequently she paid only one seventh of this sum to her own ship owners. The rest $350,000, she paid to Northern ship owners; and this was the amount of the drain from the South, occasioned by the monopoly of the indirect trade.

All foreign ships entering our ports, have to pay fifty cents a ton as "light money." The tonnage of the foreign ships which entered our ports in the year ending the 30th of June, 1860, was 2,540,387 tons. Fifty cents a ton on this is $1,270,000. It is impossible [to determine] how much this tax enabled American vessels to increase their charges for freight. As far as it operated at all, it operated as a discriminating duty in their favor, the amount of which was paid to them by the consumer of the goods imported by them, and was a drain from the South, to the extent that she was a consumer. Let it pass.

The annual amount of the fishing of late, has been about $450,000. This money goes out of the public treasury, of which the South has at least an interest of one-third. Therefore the drain from this source was $130,000.

The number of fugitive slaves escaping from the South is by the census of 1850 ten or twelve hundred; count them at eleven hundred. These slaves are almost always choice slaves, and in the prime of life. It is safe therefore to value them at $1,000 each. The drain then from this source was $1,100,000.

For the year ending the 30th of June 1859, the amount of foreign goods consumed was $318,000,000. Of these the South on the criterion aforesaid, of ability to consume, consumed one-third, or $106,000,000. The amount of foreign goods imported directly into the South, was, say $33,000,000. Of which $1,000,000 [was] exported. So that 32,000,000 was a part of the $106,000,000 which was imported directly into the South. Consequently the rest, $74,000,000, must have come to the South by the way of the North.

Now the cost of bringing these goods from the North to the South was an unnecessary addition to the cost of bringing them to the North from Europe. They might as well have come directly to the South. Consequently the price paid for bringing them from the North to the South was a mere bounty to the carriers and others engaged in the business. What was the amount of this price—what was the cost of transporting them from the North to the South? It was, according to my estimate, as much as seven per cent. of their value; therefore the cost was $5,180,000. The shipping engaged in the transportation, belonged nearly four-fifths to the North, and a little over one-fifth to the South. Consequently the amount paid to the North was, say $4,000,000. This amount was the drain from this source.

If we make productions or population the test, the part of the public money expended at the South ought to be at least one-third. The expenditures for the year ending 30th June, 1858, were $83,751,000, of which one-third is $27,900,000. This then is the amount that ought to have been spent in the South. The amount actually spent there, according to the best estimates I have seen, was only one-fifth, whilst the rest, four-fifths, was spent at the North. It is true that a considerable part of the expenditure was in the payment of the public debt. But why is it that the public creditors happen to be mostly at the North[?] Merely because the working of the Federal Government has been such as to cause capital to accumulate at the North, while none can accumulate at the South. The difference between one-fifth and one-third of $83,751,000 is $11,166,000. This last sum was the drain by the excess of expenditure at the North.

Mr. Kettel, in his late work entitled "Southern wealth and Northern profits,"[12] puts down the number of Southern persons annually travelling at fifty thousand, and the amount they

---

12. Thomas Prentice Kettell, a northern Democrat and late editor of the *Democratic Review,* published his *Southern Wealth and Northern Profits* in New York in 1860. The book urged a conciliatory northern policy towards the South, for the two sections were economically interdependent, and disunion would ruin northern prosperity.

spend there at $1000 per head. I think it will be safe then to say that the amount spent by them there was $25,000,000, half of his estimate.

Now, how much of value does the South receive in return for this sum[?] A few articles of clothing and of show is all these persons bring back with them. Those articles, and the exemption from supporting them while they are at the North, is all the South gets in return for these $25,000,000. Suppose we allow $10,000,000 for these items, then the amount drained out of the South in this way will be $15,000,000.

In addition to the above drains, there is another for which I have no data. Many Northern men are mere sojourners in the South. These send their earnings to the North. Many others live at the North, but have houses or branch houses at the South.

TO SUM UP—DRAINS

By the Tariff,	$50,000,000
By the Coasting Trade,	3,200,000
By the Indirect Trade,	350,000
By the Fishing Bounties,	150,000
By the Fugitive Slaves,	1,100,000
By the South's Foreign Goods Coming VIA North,	4,000,000
By the Excess of Public Expenditures at North,	$11,166,000
By the Southern Travel at North,	15,000,000–$84,966,000

Eighty-five millions is the amount of the drains from the South to the North in one year,—drains in return for which the South receives nothing. But this is not all. Some of these drains have been in operation almost from the beginning of the Government, in 1789, and the others for a long time. How enormous, then, must be the amount for the whole period during which they have been in operation. Can we not approximate that amount? I think we may. The relation which the drains for the whole period bear to the revenue from customs for the whole period, will be much the same as the relation which the drains for any one year bear to the revenue from customs of that year. We have in the financial report of the Treasury, the amount of revenue collected from customs, from 1789 to 1859; that amount is $1,482,382,942. The amount of revenue from customs, in 1859, was within a fraction of $50,000,000. Consequently, the amount of the drains during the whole must, according to this rule, have been over $2,500,000,000.

This is not all. There is interest to be counted on the drains, interest on each year's drains from that year down to this. For if the money had remained at the South, it would, it is to be presumed, have been put to use and made interest at the rate common in the South, seven or eight per cent. Adding interest, we shall have another sum almost, I dare say, equal to the principal; I have not made the tedious calculation.

Let us, however, to be within bounds throw away $500,000,000 of the principal so as to leave that $2,000,000,000, and put the interest down at the same sum; then the gross sum of principal and interest will be four thousand millions of dollars.

This is what the South has paid to the North without any return for it, since the foundation of the government under the operation of the Union; a sum equal I believe to the valuation of all the property of the North in 1850, as given in the census of that year. And the North reproaches the South with its poverty, and points the finger of compassion at her worn out fields, her tumble down houses, her decaying villages and her sparse population. Could any other people in the world have stood this drain and live? What would they have been, had this money been kept at home and there put to use! Only think what the South would of necesity [sic], now be in commerce, in manufactures, in agriculture, in art, in science, in literature, in every thing, that makes civilization if she were now worth $4,000,000,000, more than she is.

And this drain, goes on increasing every year with the increase of the manufactures of the North and the increase of the capacity of the South to consume. And these are increasing at a great rate. The production of cotton alone, is augmenting at the rate of five [per] cent a year for the last decade. Thus, if, in 1860, there will be four millions of bales made, in 1870, there will be six millions, in 1880, nine millions. Supposing the rate shall not continue, yet we are certain that the increase will be at a great rate.

We may now form some estimate of what the South would gain by a separation from the North, for [by] the mere act of separation all these drains would stop running, and the golden waters be retained within her own borders. And the grand option would be presented to her of adopting perfect free trade, by which her consumers would gain eighty millions a year clear money in the consequent lower price at which they could purchase their goods or a system of protection to her own mechanics and artisans and manufactures by which they would soon come to rival the best in the world. Such a system as England had to resort to before her manufactures had taken root.

The statistics and figures which I have presented, I of course only offer as approximations. But I feel sure that I may say that they prove at least this much; that the drain of money and property going on from the North to the South is astoundingly great.[13] It is most certain that the gain to the South, to result from cutting of this drain would exceed almost beyond comparison the losses she would sustain.

There is another point to which I call your attention. I hear it said that there is no cause sufficient to justify a separation at this time. Is that true? Now it is a principle of law announced

13. Benning, of course, means from the South to the North.

by Mr. Webster in his speech at Capon Springs in 1851,[14] and indeed held by all lawyers, that a bargain broken on one side is broken on all sides. And at least nine if not thirteen of the Northern States have broken the compact of the Constitution. They have refused to carry out the provision in that instrument, which requires the surrender of fugitive slaves, and if they have violated it in one particular it makes out our *title;* it makes our *right* to the separation perfect. We have already shown on other grounds that it is expedient—nay, indispensable to our existence.

But I go further, gentlemen, and deny that the election of Mr. Lincoln was not an overt, or to speak in their own language an unconstitutional act. I question that—I venture to question it come from what source it may. The Constitution says in the preamble, that it was made to form a more perfect Union, to establish justice and to insure domestic tranquility. The intent of the Black Republican Party in electing Mr. Lincoln was to make a less perfect union, to establish injustice, and to organize domestic strife. The intent with which he was elected, was, therefore, directly in the teeth of the *intent* of the Constitution, and I say, that this is sufficiently unconstitutional for me. [Cheers.]

But I take higher ground. I say, gentlemen, that it may happen that we will not be bound to stay in this Union, although there may not have been a violation of the Constitution. I say there may be a case where we would have a right to go out of the Union without an unconstitutional act having been perpetrated; and I think when I have stated the case you will

14. In his speech at Capon Springs, Virginia, on June 28, 1851, United States Senator Daniel Webster of Massachusetts, despite his reverence for Union, conceded "that if the Northern States refuse, willfully and deliberately, to carry into effect that part of the Constitution which respects the restoration of fugitive slaves, and Congress provide no remedy, the South would no longer be bound to observe the compact. [Immense applause]. A bargain cannot be broken on one side and still bind the other side." *Speeches of Mr. Webster at Capon Springs, Virginia . . . June 28, 1851* (n.p., n.d.), p. 12.

all agree with me. The Constitution provides that it may be amended in a certain way. Suppose that there should be found at the North a sufficient majority to put this clause in the Constitution, that the slaves should be set free, and their masters hung. This might be done in accordance with the very letter of the Constitution, and yet if it were done, and so to become a part of the Constitution, the South, I say, would have the right to resist it. And why? I answer, because the Creator himself has established a law which is higher than all human enactments—the law of self-preservation. [Cheers.] Our fathers could not make a Constitution which would bind their posterity in such a way that if they observed it they themselves would be utterly destroyed. Men have the right to self-preservation. God gave it to them, and man cannot deprive them of it. Indeed, I might, if I chose, take lower ground. I might insist that we are in all respects as sovereign as our fathers were, and therefore, that if they could make a Constitution for themselves, we can make another for ourselves.

These, then, are all the objections to the measure which I suggest as a remedy for the evils under which we live. I ask you in soberness, in candor, if the objections are sufficient to outweigh the horrors of abolition, and the enormous pressure of those laws to which I have referred. I know that you will agree with me that they are not. Why, then, will you not disregard the objections and adopt that remedy? Is there any other course left to you? If so, what is it? But surely there is none. Why hesitate? the question is between life and death.

Well, if these things be so, let us do our duty; and what is our duty? I say, men of Georgia, let us lift up our voices and shout, "Ho! for independence!" [Prolonged applause.] Let us follow the example of our ancestors, and prove ourselves worthy sons of worthy sires!

7

Joseph E. Brown's Secessionist Public Letter, December 7, from Milledgeville

The other six protagonists in the Milledgeville showdown can be usefully compared. The seventh, Joseph E. Brown, was a breed apart. Yet this unique ruler illuminated an important characteristic of the conventional establishment. Brown showed that the right nonslaveholder could triumph within the slaveholders' inner circle.

Raised in a hard-scrabble region of North Georgia and a rural day laborer as a lad, Brown acted out an authentic American Horatio Alger story. He would repeatedly borrow barely enough money for a term's schooling in South Carolina, excel at the out-of-state secondary academy, come home to work off the loan, borrow again, leave for school again, excel again, come home to work again. The exhausting process finally culminated in his graduation from Yale Law School. He did not stay for the graduation ceremony, lest he miss a money-making day back home.

At twenty-four years old, the Yale graduate began his career tardily, compared with lawyer/political aspirants from more af-

fluent Georgia families. Brown quickly caught up. He was state senator at age twenty-eight, presidential elector at thirty, judge at thirty-three and then, at thirty-six, the Democrats' candidate for governor in 1857, the little-known darkhorse nominee of a bitterly divided state Democratic Party convention. Although mocked as "the ploughboy" candidate, Brown defeated Benjamin H. Hill. He won re-election in 1859, 1861, and 1863.

As pre-Civil War governor, Brown gained grudging respect from his "betters," who had expected the "ploughboy" to defer to them. But only with this December 7, 1860, public letter from Milledgeville did Brown begin to command the Georgia ruling class. And the best was yet to come. Joseph E. Brown would imminently transcend all these debaters, first as Georgia's Civil War governor, then in a sensational postwar career as United States Senator, railroad tycoon, and member of Georgia's ruling "Bourbon Triumvirate."[1]

Gentlemen: Your letter requesting me to give to the people of Georgia my views upon the issues involved in the election of delegates to the State Convention, which is to assemble in January next, has been received.

Such is the extent of my official labors at present, that I can devote but little time to the preparation of a reply. If, however, any importance is attached to my opinions, in the present perilous times, I cheerfully give them to my fellow citizens. I propose to discuss briefly three propositions.

1st. Is the election of Mr. Lincoln to the Presidency, sufficient cause to justify Georgia and the other Southern States in seceding from the Union?

---

1. The best biography is Joseph H. Parks, *Joseph E. Brown of Georgia* (Baton Rouge, 1976). We have transcribed Brown's public letter from *The* (Milledgeville Weekly) *Federal Union,* December 11, 1860.

2d. What will be the results to the institution of slavery which will follow submission to the inauguration and administration of Mr. Lincoln as the President of one section of the Union?

3d. What will be the effect which the abolition of Slavery will have upon the interests and the social position of the large class of nonslaveholders and poor white laborers, who are in the South?

First, is the election of Mr. Lincoln sufficient cause to justify the secession of the Southern States from the Union? In my opinion the election of Mr. Lincoln, viewed only in the light of the triumph of a successful candidate, is not sufficient cause for a dissolution of the Union. This, however, is a very contracted and narrow view of the question. Mr. Lincoln is a mere mote in the great political atmosphere of the country, which, as it floats, only shows the direction in which the wind blows. He is the mere representative of a fanatical abolition sentiment—the mere instrument of a great triumphant political party, the principles of which are deadly hostile to the institution of Slavery, and openly at war with the fundamental doctrines of the Constitution of the United States. The rights of the South, and the institution of slavery, are not endangered by the triumph of Mr. Lincoln, as a man; but they are in imininent danger from the triumph of the powerful party which he represents, and of the fanatical abolition sentiment which brought him into power, as the candidate of the Northern section of the Union, over the united opposition of the Southern section against him. The party embracing that sentiment, has constantly denied, and still denies, our equality in the Union, and our right to hold our slaves as property; and avows its purpose to take from us our property, so soon as it has the power. Its ability to elect Mr. Lincoln as its candidate, shows it now has the power to control the Executive branch of the Government. As the President, with the advice and consent of the Senate, appoints the Judges of the Supreme Court of the

United States, when vacancies occur, its control of the Executive power will, in a few years, give it the control of the Judicial Department; while the constant increase of abolition sentiment, in the Northern States, now largely in the majority in Congress, together with the admission of other free States, will very soon, give it the power in the Legislative Department. The whole Government will then be in the hands of our enemies. The election of Mr. Lincoln is the first great step in this programme. It is the triumph of the Northern over the Southern section of the Union: of Northern fanaticism over Southern equality and Southern rights. While, therefore, the election of Mr. Lincoln, as a man, is no sufficient cause to justify secession, the triumph of the Northern section of the Union over the Southern section, upon a platform of avowed hostility to our rights, does, in my opinion, afford ample cause to justify the South in withdrawing from a confederacy where her equality, her honor, and the rights of her people, can no longer be protected.

Second, What will be the result to the institution of slavery, which will follow submission to the inauguration and administration of Mr. Lincoln as the President of one section of the Union? My candid opinion is, that it will be the total abolition of slavery, and the utter ruin of the South, in less than twenty-five years. If we submit now, we satisfy the Northern people that, come what may, we will never resist. If Mr. Lincoln places among us his Judges, District Attorneys, Marshals, Post Masters, Custom House officers, etc., etc., by the end of his administration, with the control of these men, and the distribution of public patronage, he will have succeeded in dividing us to an extent that will destroy all our moral powers, and prepare us to tolerate the running of a Republican ticket, in most of the States of the South, in 1864. If this ticket only secured five or ten thousand votes in each of the Southern States, it would be as large as the abolition party was in the North a few years since. It would hold a ballance [sic] of power between any two

political parties into which the people of the South may hereafter be divided. This would soon give it the control of our
elections. We would then be powerless, and the abolitionists
would press forward, with a steady step, to the accomplishment
of their object. They would refuse to admit any other slave
States to the Union. They would abolish slavery in the District
of Columbia, and at the Forts, Arsenals and Dock Yards, within
the Southern States, which belong to the United States. They
would then abolish the internal slave trade between the States,
and prohibit a slave owner in Georgia from carrying his slaves
into Alabama or South Carolina, and there selling them. These
steps would be taken one at a time, cautiously, and our people
would submit. Finally, when we were sufficiently humiliated,
and sufficiently in their power, they would abolish slavery in
the States. It will not be many years before enough of free
States may be formed out of the present territories of the United
States, and admitted into the Union, to give them sufficient
strength to change the Constitution, and remove all Constitutional barriers which now deny to Congress this power. I do
not doubt, therefore, that submission to the administration of
Mr. Lincoln will result in the final abolition of slavery. If we
fail to resist now, we will never again have the strength to
resist.

3rd, What effect will the abolition of slavery have upon
the interest and social position of the large class of nonslaveholders and poor white laborers in the South? Here would
be the scene of the most misery and ruin. Probably no one is
so unjust as to say that it would be right to take from the
slaveholder his property without paying him for it. What would
it cost to do this? There are, in round numbers, 4,500,000 slaves
in the Southern States.[2] They are worth, at a low estimate, 500

2. Brown here overestimated by about 500,000 slaves, or 11 percent. The
actual number of slaves in the South in 1860 was 3,950,511 according to the
federal census of that year, which had not been published when Brown wrote.

dollars each. All will agree to this. Multiply the 4,500,000 by 500 and you have twenty-two hundred and fifty millions of dollars [$2,250,000,000], which these slaves are worth. No one would agree that it is right to rob the Southern slaveholders of this vast sum of money without compensation. The Northern States would not agree to pay their proportion of the money, and the people of the South must be taxed to raise the money. If Georgia were only an average Southern State, she would have to pay one fifteenth part of this sum, which would be $150,000,000. Georgia is much more than an average State, and she must therefore pay a larger sum. Her people now pay less than half a million of dollars a year, of tax. Suppose we had ten years within which to raise the $150,000,000, we should then have to raise, in addition to our present tax, $15,000,000 per annum, or over thirty times as much as we now pay.—The poor man, who now pays one dollar, would then have to pay $30.00. But suppose the Northern States agreed to help pay for these slaves, (who believes they would do it?) the share of Georgia would then be about one thirtieth of the twenty-two hundred and fifty millions of dollars, or over seventy-five millions; which, if raised in ten years, would be over fifteen times as much as our present tax. In this calculation, I have counted the slave-holder as taxed upon his own slaves to raise money to pay him for them. This would be great injustice to him. If the sum is to be raised by the tax upon others, the non-slaveholders and poor white men of the South, would have to pay nearly the whole of this enormous sum, out of their labor. This would load them and their children with grievous indebtedness and heavy taxes for a long time to come. But suppose we were rid of this difficulty, what shall be done with these 4,500,000 negroes, when set free? Some of the Northern States have already passed laws prohibiting free negroes from coming into their limits. They will help to harbor our runaway slaves, but will not receive among them our free negroes. They would not permit them to go there and live with them. Then

what? One may say, send them to Africa. To such a proposition
I might reply, send them to the moon. You may say that is not
practicable. It is quite as much so as it is for us to pay for and
send this vast number of negroes to Africa, with the means at
our command.

No one would be so inhuman as to propose to send them
to Africa and set them down upon a wild, naked sea coast,
without provisions for at least one year. What will it cost to
take them from their present home to Africa, and carry provisions there to keep them a single year? (if left with only one
year's supply, many of them would starve to death.) It cannot
be done for $250.00 each. At that sum it would amount to
eleven hundred and twenty-five millions of dollars
[$1,125,000,000]. Where will we get the money? Our people
must be taxed to raise it. This would be half as large a sum
as the above estimate of the value of the negroes. If the Southern States had it to raise Georgia's part would be over
$75,000,000, which added to the part of the amount to be paid
to owners for the negroes, would amount to $225,000,000;
which must be raised by taxing the people, or loading them
with a debt which would virtually enslave our whole people
for generations to come. It must be remembered that we own
no territory in Africa large enough to colonize 4,500,000 people. This too must be bought at a very heavy cost. The Northern people would not consent to be taxed to raise these
enormous sums, either to pay for the negroes, or to pay for
sending them to Africa, or to pay for land upon which to colonize them; as they do not wish to do either. They wish to take
them from their owners without pay, and set them free, and
let them remain among us. Many people at the North, say that
negroes are our fit associates; that they shall be set free, and
remain among us—intermarrying with our children, and en-
joying equal privileges with us. But suppose we were over the
difficulty of paying the owners for the negroes, and they were
taken from their masters without pay, and set free and left

among us, (which is the ultimate aim of the Black Republicans,) what would be the effect upon our society? We should
still have rich men and poor men. But few of our slave owners
have invested all they have in negroes. Take their negroes
from them unjustly, and they will many of them still be more
wealthy than their neighbors. If all were left for a time with
equal wealth, every person who has noticed man and society
knows that, in a few years, some would grow rich and others
poor. This has always been the case, and always will be. If we
had no negroes, the rich would still be in a better condition
to take care of themselves than the poor. They would still seek
the most profitable and secure investment for their capital.
What would this be? The answer suggests itself to every mind:
it would be land. The wealthy would soon buy all the lands of
the South worth cultivating. Then what? The poor would all
become tenants, as they are in England, the New England
States, and all old countries where slavery does not exist. But
I must not lose sight of the 4,500,000 free negroes to be turned
loose among us. They, too, must become tenants, with the poor
white people for they would not be able to own lands. A large
proportion of them would spend their time in idleness and vice,
and would live by stealing, robbing and plundering. Probably
one fourth of the whole number would have to be maintained
in our penitentiary, prisons, and poor houses. Our people, poor
and rich, must be taxed to pay the expense of imprisoning and
punishing them for crime. This would be a very heavy burden.
But suppose three fourths of the whole number would work
for a living. They would have to begin the world miserably
poor, with neither land, money nor provisions. They must
therefore become day laborers for their old masters, or such
others as would employ them. In this capacity they would at
once come in competition with the poor white laborers. Men
of capital would see this, and fix the price of labor accordingly.
The negro has only been accustomed to receive his victuals
and clothes for his labor. Few of them, if free, would expect

anything more. It would therefore be easy to employ them at
a sum sufficient to supply only the actual necessaries of life.
The poor white man would then go to the wealthy land-owner
and say, I wish employment. Hire me to work. I have a wife
and children who must have bread. The land-owner would offer
probably twenty cents per day. The laborer would say, I cannot
support my family on that sum. The landlord replies, That is
not my business. I am sorry for you, but I must look to my
own interest. The black man who lives on my land has as
strong an arm, and as heavy muscles as you have, and can do
as much labor. He works for me at that rate, you must work
for the same price, or I cannot employ you. The negro comes
into competition with the white man and fixes the price of his
labor, and he must take it or get no employment.

Again, the poor white man wishes to rent land from the
wealthy landlord—this landlord asks him half the crop of common upland or two thirds or even three fourths, for the best
bottom land. The poor man says this seems very hard. I cannot
make a decent support for my family at these rates. The landlord replies, here are negroes all around me anxious to take
it at these rates; I can let you have it for no less. The negro
therefore, comes into competition with the poor white man,
when he seeks to rent land on which to make his bread, or a
shelter to protect his wife and his little ones, from the cold and
from the rain; and when he seeks employment as a day laborer.
In every such case if the negro will do the work the cheapest,
he must be preferred. It is sickening to contemplate the mis-
eries of our poor white people under these circumstances. They
now get higher wages for their labor than the poor of any other
country on the globe. Most of them are land owners, and they
are now respected. They are in no sense placed down upon a
level with the negro. They are a superior race, and they feel
and know it. Abolish slavery, and you make the negroes their
equals, legally and socially (not naturally, for no human law
can change God's law) and you very soon make them all ten-

ants, and reduce their wages for daily labor to the smallest
pittance that will sustain life. Then the negro and the white
man, and their families, must labor in the field together as
equals. Their children must go to the same poor school together,
if they are educated at all. They must go to church as equals;
enter the Courts of justice as equals, sue and be sued as equals,
sit on juries together as equals, have the right to give evidence
in Court as equals, stand side by side in our military corps as
equals, enter each others' houses in social intercourse as equals;
and very soon their children must marry together as equals.
May our kind Heavenly Father avert the evil, and deliver the
poor from such a fate. So soon as the slaves were at liberty,
thousands of them would leave the cotton and rice fields in the
lower parts of our State, and make their way to the healthier
climate in the mountain region. We should have them plundering and stealing, robbing and killing, in all the lovely vallies
of the mountains. This I can never consent to see. The mountains contain the place of my nativity, the home of my manhood,
and the theatre of most of the acts of my life; and I can never
forget the condition and interest of the people who reside there.
It is true, the people there are generally poor; but they are
brave, honest, patriotic, and pure hearted. Some who do not
know them, have doubted their capacity to understand these
questions, and their patriotism and valor to defend their rights
when invaded. I know them well, and I know that no greater
mistake could be made. They love the Union of our fathers,
and would never consent to dissolve it so long as the constitution is not violated, and so long as it protects their rights;
but they love liberty and justice more; and they will never
consent to submit to abolition rule, and permit the evils to
come upon them, which must result from a continuance in the
Union when the government is in the hands of our enemies,
who will use all its power for our destruction. When it becomes
necessary to defend our rights against so foul a domination, I
would call upon the mountain boys as well as the people of the

lowlands, and they would come down like an avalanche and swarm around the flag of Georgia with a resolution that would strike terror into the ranks of the abolition cohorts of the North. Wealth is timid, and wealthy men may cry for peace, and submit to wrong for fear they may lose their money: but the poor, honest laborers of Georgia, can never consent to see slavery abolished, and submit to all the taxation, vassalage, low wages and downright degradation, which must follow. They will never take the negro's place; God forbid.

I know that some contemptible demagogues have attempted to deceive them by appealing to their prejudices, and asking them what interest they have in maintaining the rights of the wealthy slaveholder. They cannot be deceived in this way. They know that the government of our State protects their lives, their families and their property; and that every dollar the wealthy slaveholder has, may be taken by the government of the State, if need be, to protect the rights and liberties of all. One man, in a large neighborhood, has a mill. Not one in fifty has a mill. What would be thought of the public speaker who would appeal to the fifty, and ask them what interest they have in defending their neighbor's mill, if an abolition mob were trying to burn it down? Another has a store. Not one in fifty has a store. Who would say the fifty should not help the one if an invader is about to burn his store? Another has a blacksmith shop. Not one in fifty has a blacksmith shop. Shall the shop be destroyed by the common enemy and no one protect the owner because no one near, has the same peculiar kind of property? It may be that I have no horse, and you have a horse; or that I have a cow, and you have no cow. In such case, if our rights of property are assailed by a common enemy, shall we not help each other? Or I have a wife and children, and a house, and another has neither wife and children, nor house. Will he, therefore, stand by and see my house burned and my wife and children butchered, because he has none? The slaveholder has honestly invested the money, which it has cost him years of

toil to make, in slaves, which are guaranteed to him by the
laws of our State. The common enemy of the South seeks to
take the property from him. Shall all who do not own slaves,
stand by and permit it to be done? If so, they have no right to
call on the slaveholder, by taxation, or otherwise, to help protect their property or their liberties. Such a doctrine is mon-
strous; and he who would advance it, deserves to be rode upon
the sharpest edge of one of Lincoln's rails. The doctrine strikes
at the very foundation of society, and if carried out, would
destroy all property, and all protection to life, liberty and
happiness.

The present is a critical time with the people of the South.
We all, poor and rich, have a common interest, a common
destiny. It is no time to be wrangling about old party strifes.
Our common enemy, the Black Republican party, is united
and triumphant. Let us all unite. If we cannot all see alike,
let us have charity enough towards each other, to admit that
all are equally patriotic in their efforts to advance the common
cause. My honest convictions are, that we can never again
live in peace with the Northern abolitionists, unless we can
have new constitutional guarantees, which will secure our
equal rights in the Territories, and effectually stop the discussion of the slavery question in Congress, and secure the
rendition of fugitive slaves. These guarantees I do not believe
the people of the Northern States will ever give, while we
remain together in the Union. Their opinion is, that we will
always compromise away a portion of our rights, and submit,
for the sake of peace. If the Cotton States would all secede
from the Union before the inauguration of Mr. Lincoln, this
might possibly lead to a Convention of all the States, which
might terminate in a reunion with the new constitutional
guarantees necessary for our protection. If the Northern
States then failed to give these guarantees, there can be no
doubt that Virginia, Maryland, North Carolina, Delaware,
Kentucky, Missouri, and Tennessee would unite with the Cot-

ton States in a Southern Confederacy and we should form a Republic in which, under the old Constitution of our fathers, our people could live in security and peace. I know that many of our people honestly believe that it would be best to wait for these border slave States to go out with us. If we wait for this, we shall *submit;* for some of those States will not consent to go, and the North will then consent to give us no new guarantees of peace. They will say that we have again blustered and submitted, as we always do.

In my late message to the General Assembly, I recommended the enactment of retalitory [sic] laws against these Northern States which have nullified the fugitive slave law.[3] I think those laws should still be enacted. They would have been equally applicable had either of the other candidates for the Presidency been successful. Now that Mr. Lincoln is successful, they should be upon our staute [sic] book, so long as we remain in the Union. There can no longer be a reasonable doubt, that the gallant State of South Carolina will secede from the Union very soon after her Convention meets. The States of Florida, Alabama and Mississippi will follow in quick succession. While our Convention is in session, we shall probably be surrounded on every side but one, with free and independent States out of the Union. With these States, we have a common interest. Thus surrounded, shall Georgia remain under abolition rule, and refuse to unite with her sister States around her? I trust not. If so, we forfeit all claim to our proud title of Empire State of the South. Why remain? Will the Northern States repeal their personal liberty bills and do us justice? No. The Legislature of one of the nullifiing [sic] States (Vermont) has just adjourned. A bill has been introduced for the repeal of those unconstitutional and offensive laws. The question has been discussed, and it is reported that the House

3. For a discussion of Brown's Special Message of November 7, 1860, see above, pp. xi–xii.

in which the bill was introduced, has refused to pass the repealing law, by a vote of over two-thirds. This action has been
had with full knowledge of the state of things now existing in
the South, and shows a deliberate determination not to do us
justice. Is further notice to Vermont necessary? I am aware
that the fears of some have been appealed to, and they have
been told that if we secede, the United States Government
will attempt to coerce us back into the Union, and we shall
have war.

The President in his late message, while he denies our
Constitutional right to secede, admits that the General Government has no Constitutional right to coerce us back into the
Union, if we do secede.[4] Secession is not likely, therefore, to
involve us in war. Submission may. When the other States
around us secede, if we remain in the Union, thousands of our
people will leave our State, and it is feared that the standard
of revolution and rebellion may be raised among us, which
would at once involve us in civil war among ourselves. If we
must fight, in the name of all that is sacred, let us fight our
common enemy, and not fight each other.

In my opinion, our people should send their wisest and best
men to the Convention, without regard to party distinctions,
and should intrust much to their good judgment and sound
discretion, when they meet. They may, then, have new lights
before them, which we do not now have; and they should be
left free to act upon them.

My fervent prayer is, that the God of our fathers may
inspire the Convention with wisdom, and so direct their coun-

4. Brown here referred to President James Buchanan's Annual Message
to Congress, December 3, 1860. The presidential message was more ambiguous
than the Georgia governor reported. Buchanan conceded he had no authority
to coerce a *state*. But he also affirmed his power to "take care that the law be
faithfully executed"—which he could do by "coercing" a *citizen* to obey the law.
Buchanan's distinction between coercing a Georgian and coercing Georgia was
not one that the state of Georgia could have accepted.

sels as to protect our rights and preserve our liberties to the latest generation.

I am, gentlemen, with great respect,

Your fellow citizen,

JOSEPH E. BROWN

Selected Bibliography

Manuscripts

University of Georgia Library, Athens:
    Colonel David C. Barrow Papers
    Keith Read Manuscript Collection
    Telamon Cuyler Collection
    Howell Cobb Family Papers
Southern Historical Collection, Wilson Library, University of North
    Carolina at Chapel Hill:
    Thomas Butler King Papers

Newspapers (Microfilm)

The Federal Union (Milledgeville), Weekly, 1860.
The Southern Recorder (Milledgeville), Weekly, 1860.
The Southern Banner (Athens), Weekly, 1860.
The Southern Watchman (Athens), Weekly, 1860.
The Daily Constitutionalist (Augusta), 1860.
The Macon Daily Telegraph, 1860.
The Savannah Daily Republican, 1860.
The Georgia Journal and Messenger (Macon), Weekly, 1860.

Primary Sources

Benning, Henry L. *Speech on Federal Relations, November 19, 1860* (N.d., n.p.). University of Georgia Library.

Brown, Joseph E., "Letter to A.H. Colquitt. *et al.*, December 7, 1860," in *The Federal Union* (Milledgeville weekly), December 11, 1860.

————. *Special Message of Governor Joseph E. Brown to the Legislature of Georgia, on our Federal Relations, Retaliatory State Legislation, the Right of Secession, etc. November 7th, 1860.* Milledgeville: Boughton, Nisbet and Barnes, 1860.

Candler, Allen D., ed. *The Confederate Records of the State of Georgia.* Vols. 1–4, 6. Atlanta: Charles P. Byrd, State Printer, 1909–16; reprint, New York: AMS Publishing Company, 1972.

Cleveland, Henry C. *Alexander H. Stephens in Public and Private. With Letters and Speeches Before, During and Since the War.* Philadelphia: National Publishing Co., 1866.

Cobb, Howell, "Letter to the People of Georgia, December 6, 1860," in Ulrich Bonnell Phillips, ed., *The Correspondence of Robert Toombs, Alexander H. Stephens, and Howell Cobb,* Annual Report of the American Historical Association for the Year 1911, vol. 2. Washington: Government printing office, 1913, 505–16.

Cobb, Thomas R.R. *Substance of Remarks Made by Thomas R.R. Cobb, Esq., in the Hall of the House of Representatives, Monday Evening, November 12, 1860.* Atlanta: Printed by John H. Seals, 1860. University of Georgia Library.

Debates and Proceedings of the Georgia Convention, 1850. Milledgeville: Printed at the Federal Union office, 1850.

Harris, Hon. W. P. *Address Delivered Before the General Assembly of the State of Georgia, on Monday, December 17, 1860.* Milledgeville: Boughton, Nisbet and Barnes, 1860. University of Georgia Library.

Hill, Benjamin H. "Speech in Milledgeville, November 15, 1860," in Benjamin H. Hill, Jr., *Benjamin H. Hill of Georgia: His Life, Speeches and Writings.* Atlanta: T.H.P. Bloodworth, 1893, 238–50.

Iverson, Alfred. "Speech Delivered at Griffin, Georgia, July 14, 1859," in *The Federal Union* (Milledgeville weekly), July 26, 1859.

Jackson, Henry R. *Letters to the Hon. Alexander H. Stephens.* Savannah: John M. Cooper and Company, 1860. University of Georgia Library.

Jenkins, Charles J. "Address at the City Hall, December 24, 1860,"
    in *The Georgia Journal and Messenger* (Macon weekly), Jan-
    uary 2, 1861.
————. "Letter to Messrs. J.A. Williams, et al., December 12, 1860,"
    in *The Georgia Journal and Messenger* (Macon weekly), Jan-
    uary 2, 1861.
Johnson, Herschel V. "Letter to Twenty Four Members of the Georgia
    Legislature, November 16, 1860," in *The Southern Recorder*
    (Milledgeville weekly), November 27, 1860.
Kettell, Thomas Prentice. *Southern Wealth and Northern Profits.* New
    York: G. W. and J. A. Wood, 1860.
Lipscomb, Andrew A. *Substance of a Discourse Delivered Before the
    Legislature of Georgia on the Occasion of the Fast Day Appointed
    by His Excellency Joseph E. Brown, November 28, 1860.* Mil-
    ledgeville: Boughton, Nisbet and Barnes, 1860. University of
    Georgia Library.
Lumpkin, Wilson. "Letter to Hon. Asbury Hull, et al., December 14,
    1860," in *The Federal Union* (Milledgeville weekly), January
    1, 1861.
Moore, Frank, ed. *The Rebellion Record: A Diary of American Events.*
    11 vols. New York: G.P. Putnam 1861–63; D. Van Nostrand
    1864–68.
Nisbet, E.A. "Speech at Concert Hall in Macon, November 30, 1860,"
    in *The Macon Daily Telegraph,* December 12, 1860.
Phillips, Ulrich Bonnell, ed. *The Correspondence of Robert Toombs,
    Alexander H. Stephens, and Howell Cobb,* Annual Report of the
    American Historical Association for the Year 1911, vol. 2.
    Washington: Government Printing Office, 1913.
Stephens, Alexander H. *Speech before the Legislature of Georgia. De-
    livered at Milledgeville, November 14, 1860,* in Richard Malcolm
    Johnston and William Hand Browne, *Life of Alexander H. Ste-
    phens.* Philadelphia: J.B. Lippincott and Co., 1878.
Stephens, Linton. "Letter to Messrs. Lewis J. Groce, et al., December
    17, 1860," in *The Georgia Journal and Messenger* (Macon
    weekly), December 26, 1860.
Toombs, Robert A. *Speech Delivered in Milledgeville, on Tuesday Eve-
    ning, November 13, 1860, before the Legislature of Georgia* [Mil-
    ledgeville, 1860], in Moore, ed., *The Rebellion Record: A Diary
    of American Events,* Vol. 1, pp. 362–68.
————. "Letter to E.B. Pullin, *et al.,* December 13, 1860," in Ulrich

Bonnell Phillips, ed., *The Correspondence of Robert Toombs, Alexander H. Stephens, and Howell Cobb,* vol. 2, pp. 519–22.

United States Bureau of the Census. *A Century of Population Growth: From the First Census of the United States to the Twelfth,* 1790–1900. Washington: U.S. Census Office, Government Printing Office, 1909.

Walker, Francis A., comp. *The Statistics of the Population of the United States.* Washington: U.S. Census Office, Ninth Census, Government Printing Office, 1870.

Webster, Daniel. *Speech at Capon Springs, Virginia, June 28, 1851.* N.p., n.d.

Secondary Sources

Avery, I.W. *The History of the State of Georgia from 1850 to 1881.* New York: Brown and Derby, 1881.

Auer, J. Jeffrey, ed. *Antislavery and Disunion, 1858–1861: Studies in the Rhetoric of Compromise and Conflict.* New York: Harper and Row, 1963.

Bonner, James C. *Milledgeville: Georgia's Antebellum Capital.* Athens: The University of Georgia Press, 1985.

Bryan, T. Conn. "The Secession of Georgia," *The Georgia Historical Quarterly,* 31 (1947), 89–111.

Channing, Steven A. *Crisis of Fear: Secession in South Carolina.* New York: Norton, 1970.

Collins, Bruce W. "Governor Joseph E. Brown, Economic Issues, and Georgia's Road to Secession, 1857–1859," *The Georgia Historical Quarterly,* 71 (1987), 189–225.

Cobb, James C. "The Making of a Secessionist: Henry L. Benning and the Coming of the Civil War," *The Georgia Historical Quarterly,* 60 (1976), 313–23.

Coulter, E. Merton. "Alexander H. Stephens Challenges Benjamin H. Hill to a Duel," *The Georgia Historical Quarterly,* 57 (1973), 179–99.

Crawford, George B. "Cotton, Land, and Sustenance: Toward the Limits of Abundance in Late Antebellum Georgia," *The Georgia Historical Quarterly,* 72 (1988), 215–47.

Donnelly, William J. "Conspiracy or Popular Movement: The Historiography of Southern Support for Secession," *North Carolina Historical Review,* 42 (1965), 70–84.

Doyon, Roy R. and Thomas W. Hodler. "Secessionist Sentiment and Slavery: A Geographic Analysis," *The Georgia Historical Quarterly,* 73 (1989), 323–48.

Flippin, Percy Scott. *Herschel V. Johnson of Georgia: State Rights Unionist.* Richmond, Va.: The Dietz Printing Co., 1931.

Freehling, William W. "The Editorial Revolution, Virginia, and the Coming of the Civil War," *Civil War History,* 16 (1970), 64–72.

Hahn, Steven. *The Roots of Southern Populism: Yeoman Farmers and the Transformation of the Georgia Upcountry.* New York: Oxford University Press, 1983.

Harris, J. William. *Plain Folk and Gentry in a Slave Society: White Liberty and Black Slavery in Augusta's Hinterlands.* Middletown, Conn.: Wesleyan University Press, 1985.

Hill, Louise Biles. *Joseph E. Brown and the Confederacy.* Chapel Hill: University of North Carolina Press, 1939.

Johnson, Michael P. "A New Look at the Popular Vote for Delegates to the Georgia Secession Convention," *The Georgia Historical Quarterly,* 56 (1972), 259–75.

————. *Toward a Patriarchal Republic: The Secession of Georgia.* Baton Rouge: Louisianna State University Press, 1977.

Johnston, Richard M. and William Hand Browne. *The Life of Alexander H. Stephens.* Philadelphia: J.B. Lippincott and Company, 1878.

Marina, William and Joseph Stromberg. "'Truths of the Defeated': Alexander H. Stephens' Reflections of the Course of the American Republic," *Continuity,* No.9 (Fall, 1984), 121–38.

May, Robert E. "Psychobiography and Secession: The Southern Radical as Maladjusted 'Outsider'," *Civil War History,* 34 (1988), 46–69.

McCash, William B. "Thomas R. R. Cobb and the 'Better Terms' Argument," *The Georgia Historical Quarterly,* 60 (1976), 49–53.

————. *Thomas R.R. Cobb (1823–1862): The Making of a Southern Nationalist.* Macon, Georgia: Mercer University Press, 1983.

Mohr, Clarence. *On the Threshold of Freedom: Masters and Slaves in Civil War Georgia.* Athens: University of Georgia Press, 1986.

Parks, Joseph Howard. *Joseph E. Brown of Georgia.* Baton Rouge: Louisiana State University, 1976.

Pearce, Haywood J., Jr. *Benjamin H. Hill: Secession and Reconstruc-*

tion. Chicago: University of Chicago Press, 1928; reprint, New York, Negro Universities Press, 1969.

Phillips, Ulrich Bonnell. *Georgia and State Rights. A Study of the Political History of Georgia from the Revolution to the Civil War, With Particular Regards to Federal Relations,* Annual Report of the American Historical Association for the Year 1901, vol. 2. Washington: Government Printing Office, 1902.

———. *The Life of Robert Toombs.* New York: The Macmillan Company, 1913.

Ringold, May Spencer. "Robert Newman Gourdin and the '1860 Association'," *The Georgia Historical Quarterly,* 55 (1971), 501–509.

Schott, Thomas Edwin. *Alexander H. Stephens of Georgia: A Biography.* Baton Rouge: Louisiana State University Press, 1988.

Shryock, Richard H. *Georgia and the Union in 1850.* Durham, N.C.: Duke University Press, 1926.

Siegel, Fred. "Artisans and Immigrants: The Politics of Late Antebellum Georgia," *Civil War History,* 27 (1981), 221–30.

Thompson, William Y. *Robert Toombs of Georgia.* Baton Rouge: Louisiana State University Press, 1966.

Wooster, Ralph A. "The Secession of the Lower South: An Examination of Changing Interpretations," *Civil War History,* 7 (1961), 117–27.

CPSIA information can be obtained at www.ICGtesting.com
Printed in the USA
BVOW05s0219090116

432302BV00001B/3/P